THE GREAT BUSINESS SHAPE UP

GETTING YOURSELF AND YOUR BUSINESS INTO SHAPE FOR SUCCESS!

BY

MURRAY PRIESTLEY

✚

EDES PUBLISHING CO.

THE GREAT BUSINESS SHAPE UP

GETTING YOURSELF AND YOUR BUSINESS INTO SHAPE FOR SUCCESS!

By Murray Priestley

ISBN-13: 978-0-9788010-5-2
ISBN-10: 0-9788010-5-9

Made in the United States of America

Dedication

To Janne – Who keeps me in shape and without her
inspired and unwavering support this book would not
have been possible.

A Personal Invitation from Murray

Before you get started. I have something that I think will help you before you start reading this business-changing book.

From my perspective, you have made the first step in acquiring and getting to read this book. For that I thank you.

But reading alone will not make things happen. You must take action on these ideas. The Action Steps at the end of each chapter are just the minimum. What other thoughts come up from the ideas presented? How can you put them into your business? One of my mentors, T. Harv Eker says, "Rich people constantly learn and grow; Poor people think they already know".

My only caveat is that it is very easy in today's world to research and research and research. You must take action on ideas, get a result and then decide to keep it, change it or dump it.

Those who are successful are those who test A LOT! Be sure to visit http://ShapeUpForProfit.com and click on the "FREE BOOK BONUSES" to receive several valuable gifts that include:

- Templates that you can use for some of the Action steps in the book

- The Autopilot Monthly Newsletter

I invite you to attend one of our Shape-Up For Profit or Autopilot Your Business Workshops. These events will give you a fresh perspective on your business and on how you think about your business.

We get people who don't have a business yet, people who are still caught up in the day-to-day world of working for someone else, business owners, sales professionals and entrepreneurs coming along to learn new ideas and tactics that they can use immediately.

The events are fun, interactive and will have you excited to get started. You will meet other like-minded people, many of whom could become business partners, clients or lifelong friends.

These courses are so critical for you to attend, that I have decided to make your tuition FREE for a limited time. I have struck a deal with the publishers of this book to allow you to attend and bring your partner, as my guests. See the following pages for more details about this limited offer to you.

Thank you for taking time to get this far. I wish you tremendous success in your personal and business life, and I look forward to seeing you in person one day soon.

For your profits,

Murray Priestley

SPECIAL BONUS OFFER*

Shape-Up For Profit or
Autopilot Your Business
One-Day Workshop Free!

As a thank-you for acquiring and reading this book, Murray Priestley is offering the tuition for you and a business partner to attend the one-day Workshop as his complimentary guests. That's a total value of $1,994 – for free!

These guest seats must be registered and used prior to July 2009 and this offer is made on a space available basis. All seats are first come first served.

To assure your spot please register at http://ShapeUpForProfit.com immediately.

If you have no access to a computer call 1300-72-1995. Proof that you have this book will be required. When you register, there will be a simple question about a particular word on a page to enter in.

* This offer is open to all acquirers of The Great Business Shape-Up by Murray Priestley. Original proof of purchase is required. The offer is limited to the Shape-Up For Profit or Autopilot Your Business Workshops only, and your registration in the seminar is subject to availability of space and/or changes to the program schedule. The course must be completed by July 1, 2009. The value of this free admission for you and a companion is $1,994, as of April 2008. Corporate or organizational purchasers may not use one book to invite more than two people. While participants will be responsible for the travel, accommodation, meals and other expenses, the course tuition is complimentary. Participants in the workshops are under no additional financial obligation whatsoever to Portofino Asset Management or Murray Priestley. Portofino Asset Management reserves the right to refuse admission to anyone it believes may disrupt the Workshop, and to remove from the premises anyone it believes is disrupting the Workshop.

Table Of Contents

Introduction

The primary object of every business is to maximise profits. And there's barely a business in the world that couldn't unlock areas of hidden profit just by following a few rules and suggestions—some simple, some a little more difficult. This book will let you know what they are and how to use them. The key action here, however, is not "knowing" but "doing." With some of the ideas in this book, you're going to say: "I know that; that's simple stuff." You may know it, but do you do it? This book will also show you how to motivate yourself from merely knowing to doing – taking real and profitable action. There's a big difference when it comes to making business profits. After every chapter, you'll find an action plan that will help you to turn the good ideas in the chapter into operating tools that will improve your business systems and put you on the road to greater profits.

That is not to say that every idea in this book will benefit you. This program doesn't claim, nor does it pretend, to have all the answers to all your business problems. No book, course or seminar could do that. It will, however, expose you to some tried, tested, and field-proven ideas, concepts, and techniques that have worked for me and other successful business people. I've spent a lot of time and money not only studying the business literature, learning from mentors, and attending business seminars the world over, but I've also used these ideas to improve my own businesses and as a consultant to other businesses. I know that they work in the real world, and so will you as you implement them into the systems of your own business.

That's what this book is all about. It has been written

with the goal of helping you become the best you can be at what you do professionally. You'll quickly see how these ideas will help you to better service your customers and prospects, and to implement efficient systems, and from this greater profits will come.

It's easy, the ideas do work and they'll work for you. You will find that many of these ideas are easy to implement. As soon as you read and understand what the book is saying, you'll be able to put them into action immediately. Others may take a little longer to gear up, but the organisation and planning required are well within the scope of even tyro business persons putting together their first operations.

And that's important. It's hard to get a new business off-the-ground and profitable. In fact, 92.4% of new businesses will close their doors by the fifth year of their operation. If you make it past that milestone, chances are you are still treading a fine line. The irony here is that most businesses have untouched areas of hidden profits that make the difference between success and failure.

Ask yourself a couple of questions. First, are you making a decent living out of your business? Do you have a business or a job? Or are you working fifty or sixty hours or more a week for just enough to get by on? Sure, getting a business off the ground requires many sacrifices, but for how long and to what point? And is it enough just to make wages? Surely the main business goal is to increase the value of your business so that it is worth something substantial when you sell. Too many business owners are content to just make a decent income from their business with no idea how they could turn it into a valuable asset. This book will show you how it is done.

A small example will let you see why increasing profit is worth far more to you than the basic dollar value income. Let's say that your business earns a 20% margin of profit yearly. You could say you're going nicely, thank-you, and are quite happy with things as they are. Well, perhaps your income is fine, but what about the value of the business when it comes time to sell? Let's assume that your industry values your business at three times net profit, a modest assumption. That means for every dollar you add in profit, the value of your business increases by three dollars. Therefore, if you double your yearly profit, you triple the value of your business. This book will show you that this is the aim – increase the real value of your business so you have the opportunity to sell it for a large amount at some point in the future. It is a project well within the capabilities of any business person who wants the most from their business and is willing to put in a little study and implement what they learn.

To unlock the hidden profits in your business this book focuses on two main areas: marketing and systems. All businesses are really marketing businesses. Some do it well, and some do it poorly, but all must do it. Behind the marketing are the systems that make the business operate, some efficiently, some not. Some businesses SAY they have systems in-place, the truth is that most do not. Good marketing and efficient systems equal high profits. This book will explain simply how to get the most out of both areas.

I would like to emphasise how important it is to keep an open mind about the ideas that will be put forward. It's too easy to shrug them away because you may not agree, they don't fit with your personality, or because you've heard them before. For instance, if you've heard an idea before, say to yourself: "Yes, I've heard that before, but am I using it?" If not: "Why not?" OR better "How can I?" If you are currently using the idea, ask yourself, "How effectively am I at using it? How can I improve on it to make it even more effective for me and my business?" Then most importantly, ask yourself this question: "What will I do as a result of what I've learned?" Remember, it's not what you know—it's what you do that counts. Ideas are powerful. And good ideas are really important for any business. They're what keep your interest up and your business fresh and alive and growing. But they must be put into action. Only then will they make a difference in the way you do business, the results you realise, the fun you have, and the profits you make.

This action guide is full of good, practical, and usable ideas that can help make that big difference for you. But it's up to you to tailor them to your own unique situation, and more importantly, to put them into action. Knowing is the first step; doing is what it is all about.

Part I The Primary Reason Businesses Fail

EVEN though you may have been in business for years, there are some little known facts about succeeding and failing in business that you need to know.

Success rate; this fact will amaze you:

only 6.1% of small businesses fail to make it through the first year.

Despite all the myths and horror stories to the contrary, this small percentage means that most businesses survive the first year. They actually operate quite well for the most part and go on to last approximately three years.

It is the next three years that begin to separate the true successes from the failures. These next three years, from the third to the sixth, are where businesses run into rough terrain and failure can become a reality. If a business makes it to the ripe old age of ten, it falls into an elite group which is composed of only one in 25 businesses.

So what leads to these failures after the third year?

MURRAY PRIESTLEY

What are the basic reasons which cause so many
businesses to falter, fail and close their doors? The
answer to this question may surprise you... the essential
blame for this failure can be placed squarely on the
shoulders of the business owner; YOU!

That's right, over ninety percent of small businesses fail
because of the business owner or CEO!

Ninety percent! That is a phenomenal number that
most business owners don't ever know about, or even
suspect. You might think that such a large percentage
must be caused by a complex range of factors that are far
beyond your control such as international competition, or
industry slumps, and that they combine to unavoidably
spell doom and destruction for business owners. I would
like to be able to put your mind at ease and place the
blame somewhere else, like an orphan on a doorstep,
because no one wants to have such an overwhelming
failure rate be their fault, but unfortunately I can't.
In all the years I have been in the business of helping
businesses to become profitable, I have found this statistic
to be true 98% of the time.

So, with a statistic this dramatic, the problems each
owner faces must be varied and cover a wide spectrum of
issues, right? You'd think that you must have to solve the
problems of the world in order to bring this statistic down,
or someone would have addressed it by now. Again,
this is not true. The reason for the problem is simple and
largely preventable.

The primary reason for this rate of failure is that 90%
of small business owner's, or CEO's, simply lack the
necessary skills and knowledge to succeed.

In fact, a whopping 70% of failures are due to the owner not recognising or even ignoring weaknesses in the business. This is further exacerbated by not seeking help and not taking action when new information becomes available about how things can be fixed.

You would think that these overwhelming statistics should be enough to strike terror into the heart of even the most independent minded business owner. These devastating numbers should quite reasonably send them running for assistance at the first sign of business adversity, but surprisingly, only five percent of business owners will even recognise that they have any issues and ask for help. That's correct... only five out of every one hundred business owners will:

> Realize they have a problem in their business.
> Seek guidance on how to solve their problem.
> Implement the solution.

This might be puzzling except when taken in light of basic human nature which was aptly summarized by one of the greatest students of human nature of all time, Dale Carnegie.

"...I personally had to blunder through this old world for a third of a century before it even began to dawn upon me that ninety-nine times out of a hundred, people don't criticize themselves for anything, no matter how wrong it may be." --Dale Carnegie

This means that often the minuses that you have previously attributed to your business are, on closer inspection, more likely to be problems arising with you as the owner or CEO. In addition, as the business owner, you remain your business's biggest potential problem.

Now I said potential problem because, once you recognise this fact, you can address the problem before it grows into something other than potential.

Now that you are armed with this knowledge, you are probably wondering what you can do about it, how can you foil the inevitable? If you have already suspected the truth and have made an effort to improve your business, you have probably investigated business improvement books, courses and programs. But, has this given you a solution? You were probably focusing on your BUSINESS. The materials you were looking at or may have actually bought were probably all aimed at improving your BUSINESS.

These business improvement systems usually start right off by focusing on your BUSINESS and make recommendations for changes to your BUSINESS. You can see my point here. You can make all the changes you want to your business, and this is a fine approach which we get to later, but again, this is not targeting the 90% statistical root of the problem, the BUSINESS OWNER. Again, no one wants to admit that they are the cause of the problem, but until you do, or at least until you admit that you are potentially the source of future problems in your business, nothing will change. If you are sceptical of these statistics, or perhaps believe yourself infallible, and need further convincing, let me add my personal experience to the evidence.

In my work, I help businesses become more profitable, and I have found that every time I sit down with a client, either potential or actual, the discussion of their business always leads to the "a ha" moment of realisation. That's because during our conversation, something I say strikes home and the owner immediately recognises a problem

4

they either didn't know existed, or had forgotten about. They can see the solution, how it can be implemented and the positive impact it will make in their business. The solution is something that was there all along, they just needed someone to help them direct their attention in a way that would bring the solution to the forefront of their thinking.

Recently I was sitting with a client who is a mortgage broker. This client was complaining about the amount of paperwork that they had to process before they could even begin visiting and assisting clients. The banks and aggregators "require" an ever increasing amount of paperwork and compliance documentation. My analysis immediately suggested a solution which focused on outsourcing these low-value tasks. As we worked through the steps required to process the papers - it became apparent to the broker that this was indeed mundane work and could easily be outsourced. Over the next two weeks, my client developed a description of the low-value tasks and offloaded it to an offshore outsourcing company. What used to take my client 3 hours each day is now accomplished, summarised and e-mailed to him. The net result is that my client can now concentrate on real paying clients, and there is a massive reduction in frustration, which has resulted in a much happier broker.

So did the broker know what needed to be done? Maybe - but it wasn't until I spoke to him about the possibilities that it became apparent.

This is true for nearly every single business owner with whom I have conversations. They do not see or even recognize their own problems until I point out options and alternatives to their everyday business operations. I see the reality of this statistic over and over again and it is

true for 98% of the business owners I encounter.
So, what accounts for this statistic? What happens in a
business that is different after the first three years and
why is it the owner's fault? The answer is simple, it lies
in the natural progression and growth of a business.

Business Phases

What generally happens is that a business goes through
a number of relatively predictable phases. When you
first enter into business, you are in the first phase: start
up mode. Once through that, you move into the second, a
growth phase, and then maybe into a rapid growth phase,
and then a more mature phase. The chart shows these
typical phases in the evolution of a business.

Strategic	Human Assets	Core Competence	Box	Change Agent
Strategic >> Tactical	Strategic > Tactical	Tactical = Strategic	Tactical >> Strategic	Strategic = Tactical
Start-up	Early Growth	Late Growth	Mature	Decline?

For the owner or the CEO, each of these phases has its
own requirements, and the skills needed for the start up
phase may not easily translate to other phases.

6

There are always exceptions, but as a general rule, a business fails because the CEO or the owner cannot carry the business between these phases. In moving from one phase to another, it is often the owner who cannot transition between phases and as a result becomes a detriment to the business and can even jeopardize the success of the business.

To meet these challenges and change yourself from a potential problem to a strong vital leader you need to know how to recognize these phase transitions. The technical term for these transitions is infection points, or junctures where the needs of your business drive it in a new direction. Let me give you an example, in the start up phase you are generally worried about revenue, cash flow and how to pay the bills. The skills required are those that keep expenses low and ensure that bills get paid.

In the next phases, you have enough revenue to cover your fixed expenses, and you are not worried about where the money is coming from on a month to month basis. Now, however, you need more staff. The skills you need are now more human asset management. You hire staff, and then you begin to have staffing problems. Once you've acquired the skills to handle that, you can then start to build the business momentum and take on more work. However, with more clients, you begin to run into customer support problems. Once you solve these, your business really takes off, which means more staff, and the managers to manage the staff. You can see that as you move from phase to phase, your skills as a CEO are continually evolving. What you do has changed completely, and maybe you are not so good now at what you do.

In addition, when you start your business, you are

probably doing most of the work. In the next phase you are doing some of the work, but are beginning to hire other people to assume some of the workload. In the next stage, you have stepped away from the grunt work, but now you need to be a motivator to make sure that everybody stays on the same track. You must be the one with the vision and inspire others to support your vision

The range of skills necessary to transition a business through the various stages is daunting at the very least. How often have you heard, that an owner is a detail kind of person, or a people person, or a creative type. As a business owner, you learn the strengths and skills of your staff and you employ them as effectively as possible to maximize their efficiency. You don't expect an employee who is a stickler for details to suddenly be able to ignore them. Yet, this is exactly what is expected of a business owner or CEO. The odds of a business owner being able to lead a business through all the phases is approximately thirty percent which means that about 70% of the time, according to the research studies, businesses will fail.

How often have you heard of companies that replace the CEO with a new person and suddenly the business sky-rockets? Within six to twelve months it is a completely different company. What happened is that the new CEO suits the new business phase in a way the old CEO could not, although he might have been excellent in the previous phases.

This can often be seen in the turn-around industry. The first thing that you generally do with an ailing company is replace the existing management team, the concept being that the team that got the business into trouble, is unlikely to be the same team that can get the business out.

2

From Problem to Success
– How to Change

SO what can you do to change yourself from a potential problem into a successful owner or CEO? First of all, let's look again at what we have learned from all the businesses that have failed in the past, and let's look at this closely.

The primary reason for this rate of failure is that 90% of small business owner's, or CEO's, simply lack the necessary skills and knowledge to succeed. (Source: Dunn & Bradstreet)

In fact, a whopping 70% of failures are due to the owner not recognising or even ignoring weaknesses in the business. This is further exacerbated by not seeking help and not taking action when new information becomes available about how things can be fixed. (Source: SCORE & US Bank)

The reasons for failure:

No. 1 - Lack of skills and knowledge
No. 2 - Not recognising or ignoring weaknesses
No. 3 - Not seeking help
No. 4 - Not taking action

All these failures are serious of course, but the most important failure, the most crucial to business success is No. 4 – Not taking action. You can have all the skill and knowledge in the world, you can know exactly what is wrong with your business, you can even know how to fix it, but if you do nothing, there will be no change.

Because taking action is so critical, I am going to concentrate on this first, and then we will introduce solutions for the other problems, but unless you take action, you are doomed to failure. You may find this statement negative and harsh, but it is true. Words without action mean nothing, solutions without implementation solve nothing, knowledge without application is useless.

Taking action requires that you find out how to motivate yourself to change.

The key word here is CHANGE. And the secret to instituting change lies in you compelling yourself to change. Just thinking that you need to change is not enough. You need to reach down inside yourself and find what is truly important, what you really care about and use that to drive yourself to action. When you know your own deep secret passions, you can use it to spur yourself into taking the necessary actions in your life and in your business to improve.

Why do you need to do this? Isn't it enough to just want to change? Well, sometimes... but change goes against human nature. We like predictability and do not want to step outside the realm of our comfort zone into uncharted waters. We are often afraid. We fear the unknown. We fear the criticism of our family, friends and peers. We fear failure. However, if we know that by not changing we are headed for almost certain failure, we have the right reasons to take action.

Sometimes just the knowledge that most businesses fail because the owner or CEO fails to take action, can be enough to influence us to change, but we know statistically, this is only about 5% of the time. Do you want to count on being decidedly in the 5%, or do you want to tip the scales more in your favour and guarantee that you will make the changes necessary? To move yourself over onto the guarantee side, you need to be sure that you will take the actions necessary to make you and your business a success.

This requires massive leverage on your behaviour. This leverage is achieved through finding out what will motivate you to initiate action and what will continue to motivate you over time. What will absolutely insure that you will carry out the game plan that you set out to achieve? The answer to this question is not easy. One person's motivations differ from another's. You need to find your own unique catalyst. You may think finding your catalyst to action is simple, but often people find that what they think is important to them actually has little effect in forcing them to make a change. Remember, it takes massive leverage to sustain change over time. You need to find your passion. What excites you and makes you want to get up in the morning? These passions need to be identified and used to help you achieve your goals.

What Motivates You to Take Action?

Now, what do you really want? Project this thought into the future. What do you want in one year, five years, ten years and twenty years? You've probably thought about this a great deal already. It is usually the picture that you had in your mind when you first thought of your business. What is that image? Is it a fancy executive office on the top floor of a tall office building, or the vision of a large yacht with you and your family relaxing on the deck? It might just be a remote cabin in the country and an obscene amount of money piled up in a few banks somewhere. You may not have ever confessed it to anyone, but it is your fondest wish and the underlying expectation of what you have always dreamed your business could provide you.

The Passion Test

An additional way to help you decide what you truly want and what will ultimately motivate you to make it happen is the Passion Test. The Passion Test comes from the book of the same name by Janet and Chris Attwood. The Passion Test is simply a tool to help you determine your passions. This is what drives you, so it even comes before vision. You might have a vision to achieve certain things, but unless you are driven by your passions to achieve that vision, or choose a vision derived from your passions, you will find that you easily run out of the energy needed to reach that visionary goal.

So I highly recommend The Passion Test as a book, which provides the exercises that will help you get that process started.

Know What You Want – Setting Goals

"The #1 reason that people do not get what they want, is because they don't know what they want" -T Harv Eker

The next step is to set the direction for your actions, or to set your goals. Taking action without a clear cut direction is not much better than taking no action at all so this is an important task. Use your passions to help set your direction and convert what you are passionate about into words. Put what you ultimately want as your long term over-riding goal, keeping in mind what drives you. This is your vision. You need to ask yourself such questions as:

> How do you as the key person in your business see yourself?
> What does your vision of the future look like?
> What do you want to be able to do?
> What do you want to be able to get out of your business?

This is slightly different from the vision for the business itself. The business will have a number of goals which we will get to later, but your goals, what you personally want to get out of it, are different. Your reasons will motivate and drive you to do what needs to be done in order for your company to reach its goals. That is why, what you want is so important.

Know yourself and exactly what you want and expect out of your life and your business. So many people enter into business and spend years in that environment without having any idea of what they want, or what it is possible to get out of their business. Many business owners even put their personal lives on hold, ignoring their family and other aspects of their life for the sake of their business.

"I'm doing this for you..." is a common reply to complaints that you are not spending enough time with your loved ones.

In fact, most business owners are working so hard in their businesses that they don't have time to work on them. As a result, they've become slaves to their business. It's all backwards. They're working for their business and their family is sacrificing for their business rather than their business working for them and providing a great lifestyle.

Take the time to carefully analyse where you've come from, where you are now, and what you want to accomplish in your life and in your business. Then begin to set some meaningful goals to help you accomplish your objectives. I have included some exercises to help you set your goals at the end of this chapter. If you don't know where you want to go, you'll have no idea of what to do in order to get there.

Meaningful goals are an essential requirement for success in your personal life and in your business. With goals, you have a target to aim for, a purpose for being, and a direction to travel. Without goals, it's easy to wander aimlessly, getting sidetracked with any little thing that comes along.   It is also easy to leave out important aspects of your life so that you have no balance between work and your personal life.

When you set your goals, think of the word, "SMART." You should have SMART goals. That is, your goals should be:

- Specific
- Measurable
- Attainable
- Timebound

Specific

It is important for your goals to be Specific, so you will know exactly what you're shooting for. Your goal should be clearly defined and identified so you not only know what you are trying to accomplish, you'll also know when you achieve it.

Just to say you want more free time to spend with your family, or that you want to sell more products, merchandise or services or reduce the number of contacts to close a sale isn't enough. You need to clearly specify your goal. Is it two hours of spare time per day to spend with your family, or 12 more sales per month? A weekend away with family, or an extra $100,000 in monthly sales? How about a certain amount of certain types of products or services? How much – specifically?

Whatever your goal, there should be no doubt about what you wish to accomplish.

Measurable

Your goals should be Measurable. That is, there should be a system, or method of determining how you are progressing in your efforts for attainment. By clearly defining your goals as discussed in the previous step, you will be more able to measure them. It's important for you to be able to see your current status, as well as progression towards your goals.

Attainable

Next, your goals should be Attainable. If your goal is too high, if there's no hope for you to reach it, it won't take long for you to become discouraged. You will either lose the concentration and drive necessary to pursue your goal, or you will abandon it altogether. Then, because of your negative image of yourself relative to setting goals, you will likely give up setting goals in the future. It's a self-fulfilling mechanism.

Therefore, your goal should be something you can reach with just a little extra effort.
The key to being good at setting and achieving goals is to be realistic in your expectations. Set attainable and realistic goals that can be reached with a small amount of effort. That builds a success image, and enhances your self confidence in a positive way. Then, the next time, set a little higher goal. Not much higher, just a little higher. Again, one that you know you can achieve. And that adds on to, and builds your confidence, that much more.

Timebound

The next step is to make your goals, Timebound. That is, you should set a time limit for their attainment. This helps you keep on target, not be distracted, and encourages you to complete something you've started. Not only will this help you to realise success at a pre-designated time, but you will enhance your self-image by accomplishing your goal.

Say for instance, your goal is to take your family on vacation this year for the first time since you've gone into business. To make it easier, break that goal down into what you can do each month, each week, and even each day, if necessary. A large goal becomes much more manageable in small pieces. The key is to break specific goals into attainable and measurable bite-size pieces, and place a time deadline on them, for their accomplishment.

Focusing on Your Goals

One secret to implementing real change and reaching your goals is simply focusing on something. The more you focus on something, the greater chance you have of achieving it. So an important personal quality that you need to develop is the ability to focus. Many people hesitate to go into business because they think they lack the talents and abilities necessary to succeed. They look at others who are successful and think that they must have unique talents or capabilities. That is seldom the case. The main difference is that the successful person has developed the ability to focus. A person of average intelligence, who is focused on a clearly identified and specific goal, will consistently outperform the brightest people who are not focused on anything specific.

Law of Attraction

You may have heard of the movie called "The Secret." It was produced by an Australian woman named Ronda Burn. What the secret really highlighted is the Law of Attraction. The idea behind this "law" comes from the book called "The Science of Getting Rich" by Wallace D. Wattles. An interpretation of this law is that, if you focus hard on something, often as not it will come to be. It is not magic and you will find that if you focus on something and say: "This is what I want. Here is what I want and I can see it; almost touch it," and you continue to focus on it and you continue to do things that help you progress towards it, you will get it. That is my interpretation of the Law of Attraction.

However, you cannot just sit there and meditate and visualize something and have it magically appear; that is not going to work. What the movie failed to convey is that the hard focus must be accompanied by action. Focusing on what you want will reveal opportunities by which you might achieve your goal, but only by actually doing something about it will that goal be realized.

Looked at this way, the Law of Attraction is really powerful. The key is: know what you want, visualize exactly how you want it and then, when opportunities come up that help you progress towards getting what you want, take them. It is as simple as that.

Take Action Exercises

Throughout this book there are going to be exercises that I want you to do. It is very important to get the thinking out of your head and committing to paper. Just that simple process puts you far in front of most people and greatly increases the probability that you will actually do something. This is the first step toward real change, so decide now that you are going to make that change. Remember, just wanting something is not enough if you are going to contribute to the solution and not be a potential problem for your business, you need to take ACTION. So commit to going through the rest of this book and doing the exercises. Try them out, test them out and see what happens. You'll be really surprised how well it works.

So grab a piece of paper and pen now and start the process.

Exercise 1 – 101 Goals

The first exercise that I recommend for helping you to determine your goals comes from Mark Victor Hansen and Jack Canfield. It is called the 101 goals. Goals encompass the things you want to achieve, the person you would like to be, the experiences you would like to have, and the things you would like to own. The exercise is to simply write down those 101 goals.

Some might do this easily in a day, others it will take a little longer. It doesn't matter; the idea is to get a focus on what it really is that you want out of life and are passionate about. I heard Jack Canfield explain this exercise. "Without a doubt," he said, "anyone who does this exercise is forced to think about what they want and why." Not only that, he also said that the majority of those 101 things listed were often able to be achieved in a relatively short period of time simply because they had been written down and focused on.

Remember the Passion Test. For a goal to have a truly motivating influence, it must excite you at a very primitive level. If you have the image in your mind of cruising the world in your own yacht and relaxing on the deck in exotic locations, you will not be motivated by the goal of having a penthouse office in a fancy office building. You will not be motivated to work hard for something that you don't really want.

By the simple act of writing down 101 goals, the sheer number will also go a long way toward revealing what you truly want.

Exercise 2 – 90 day Goal Focus

Your next exercise will put those 101 goals into action. Pick three goals that you can measure, three goals that you are able to achieve, say, in the next 90 days. These are goals for you. They are not goals for the company, so choose ones that are exciting to the point that the thought of working on them motivates you. Write them down on a separate paper that you can carry with you and then make sure that you look at those goals every single day for the next 90 days and spend at least 20% of your day working and achieving those goals.

Successful people are the ones who do things. All the thinking, talking, and planning comes to nothing without execution. That is what really counts, and I believe in that so strongly that there is a chapter all about execution.

This last exercise illustrates one of the basic tenets of this book. Don't believe anything, even what is said in this book, until you have tested it. If you like that result and you think that it is heading in the right direction then continue to do it.

So pick three goals, just three. Look at them everyday and spend 20% of your day making sure that you are doing something to get those goals going.

I would put it to you now that you have a great chance that you will achieve those goals well before the 90-day mark.

Exercise 3 – The 3 Circles

The 3 Circles is simply a Venn diagram, an interlocking three circles you see on this page. You will see that all three of them interconnect in the middle at what I call the switch spot.

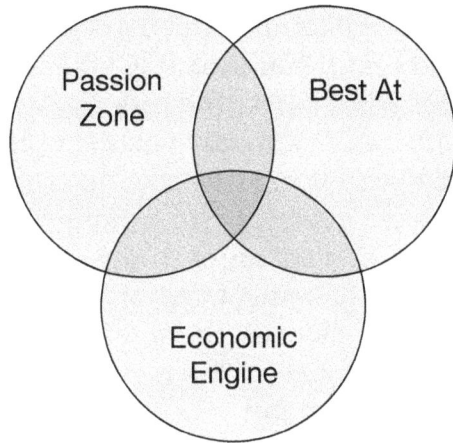

Write the particular things that you do or would like to do in each of the circles. In the first circle, write down all the things that you could be passionate about. Now notice I said, "Could be." There will be things that you definitely are passionate about, but there are also things that you could be passionate about, but aren't quite sure yet.

In the next circle, write down the things that you are good or best at.

In the last circle, write down the things that drive you to earn more money.

You can see what is going to happen here. If you can find the area of overlap between what you are passionate about, what you are good at, and what will make money, you will quickly begin to see how you should be shaping your business life. This may not be done quickly, but it is something you can come back to over and over with different ideas until something clicks. You will see that this is quite a powerful exercise.

Exercise 4: Self-Esteem Boost

It is a given that the more successful you are, the more successful you probably will be. Success breeds success. But what starts the process; what is the secret? You must have a goodly portion of high self-esteem right from the beginning. It works like this. Those with high self-esteem generally take more risks, and if you take more risks, you try more things and have a greater statistical chance of being successful at some of them. Those with low self-esteem, those who fear failing or fear what others might say about them, may not fail because they never do anything to fail at. Unfortunately, you can't manufacture high self-esteem out of thin air, so how do you come by it?

A gentleman by the name of Bill Bartman, a billionaire in the US, suggests a simple exercise to make you begin to feel better about yourself and your accomplishments. Most everyone has a range of things that they have accomplished in their life that they feel good about. Right from the earliest school days, through your working and social life there are things your have done that give you a sense of pride. Take the time now to write down a list of what you have accomplished in your life. Keep that list handy and look at it every now and again just to remind yourself that you have accomplished these things. That simple exercise will make you feel better. If you feel better, it will help to improve your self-esteem.

3
Being a Better Business Owner

YOU have discovered what motivates you at a level that will drive you to action. You have determined the direction that you want to go and are headed there. Now let's turn our attention to addressing the other reasons for failure: Lack of skills and knowledge. You can concentrate on improving your skills and knowledge in a number of ways. In addition, you can adopt successful behaviours and habits. These are ways of thinking, ways of doing things, and ways of managing your time every day that when implemented, help lead to success.

To start, in order to be a better business owner or CEO, there are several things you can do to virtually guarantee success. First, you need to be able to think clearly about your life and your business and spend some time strategising and planning. No one else is in a position to do this, so by failing to take the time to do this yourself it will not get accomplished and your business and your life will languish for lack of this direction. You also need to examine the use of your time and how to best apply it to contribute to your success. You do this through examining your particular talents and whether or not you are using them effectively. There are also numerous strategies of successful people that you can adopt as your own and benefit from implementing their techniques and philosophies.

Your Strengths

Everybody is born with things that they just naturally do well and things that they naturally don't do well. For instance, I am very good at getting projects started, taking an idea and turning it into something deliverable. What I am not very good at is the detail work needed to make a project work completely. Because I am aware of that failing, I concentrate on doing what I am good at, and I get other people to do what I am not good at.

There is a huge lesson here. If you focus your energies on trying to improve what you are not good at, you will only waste your valuable time and get frustrated. Instead use others who can do what you can't, and concentrate on improving your strengths. You will generally progress much faster.

It is so much easier during these Internet times, when it is quite simple to engage virtual assistance from all around the world for often far lower wages than you would pay at home. Why would you want to do what you are not good at? One of the things that we will cover in this book is how to engage and get work done with virtual assistance, but generally the point simply is: understand what you are good at and what you are not good at, and hire somebody else to do the latter.

Relaxing

If you are anything like me, you get your best ideas just before you go to sleep or when you are in the shower.

There is a reason for that; it is because you are in a relaxed state and your mind is free of directed thought. New ideas are difficult to formulate if your mind is already engaged in structured thought. That is why most if not all of your great ideas will come when you are in a relaxed state. In a way, your most productive time can manifest during your least productive time.

A saying that illustrates this is:

"Do not think when you are working. And do not work when you are thinking."

Thinking is about taking time out for planning and considering what you are going to do. Perhaps considering how you are going to solve a particular problem, or planning for the future. That is thinking time. Working time is when you are doing things: looking at what is happening with the business, helping with operations, actually developing the products, or whatever you might actually be doing. Try and spend your 'thinking' time separately to your 'doing' time

When you are working, do not pause in the middle of working and try and consider something else. You would better off getting up from your desk, going somewhere else, and then spending a little bit of time doing the thinking. That is a great tip that works for me. It is very easy in this ubiquitous communication age to be bombarded with a host of messages: email, instant messages, text messages, mobile telephones, radio, TV, and people wanting things. It makes it increasingly difficult to focus on any one thing. If you want to be productive, you need to focus on one thing at a time. To best do that segregate what you are doing. I block out some time in my diary to do a particular piece of work and I let no one interrupt me. I get things done and I get them done faster.

The same goes for thinking time. Again, block out a piece of time in your diary to say: "I am going to sit and plan and think." This is an unbelievably useful tip. Always set time aside in your diary to think and plan. You will soon realize how important this is to the smooth working of your business. Sure you are going to have to allow time for interruptions for doing whatever comes up day-to-day, but, the more that you can pre-plan your time to get work done, the more efficient you will be. So try it; there is an exercise. Try and chunk out some time for thinking everyday or every week, and see what happens.

Personal Traits of Exceptional Performers

What makes some business people more successful than others? I'll tell you a story to illustrate.

Some time back a friend of mine had dinner with his friend Earl Nightingale, the famous radio personality and producer of self improvement cassette programs. Earl made his life's work studying successful people and how they achieved their successes. My friend had long admired Earl for his ideas and philosophy.

On that occasion, my friend asked him what advice he would give his young son if he had one. What, based on his vast experience and knowledge, would be the prime thing that would help his son ensure success both in business as well as in his personal life.

Earl said told my friend, "You know, I have often thought about that very question. And after all the years and all the study, I've come to the conclusion that your success in life, or in business for that matter, can be boiled down to one thing. That is, your rewards will always be in direct proportion to the amount of service you render.

"You only have to look around," he said. "The people who serve others, prosper. The people who don't serve others, don't prosper. And you can tell just how successful a person is by the amount of service they render to others.

"The problem," he continued, "is that unsuccessful people either haven't learned that great secret, or they don't apply it. The successful people are the ones who develop the habits of doing the things that unsuccessful people don't do for one reason or another."

What Failures Don't Like to Do

Earl's comments hit my friend like a big hammer that night, as he realised how true they were. The more you serve your customers, and help them satisfy their needs, the more you will prosper.

And as a business owner, business manager, professional person or entrepreneur, serving your customer's needs effectively means that you must do the things that unsuccessful business owners, managers, professionals, and entrepreneurs don't do. The things that those unsuccessful people don't do are the things that most of us don't like to do either.

There is no doubt that it is difficult to work long hours or on weekends when your family is waiting for you at home, and only have a couple of "shoppers" stop by or be stood up for an appointment someone made with you.

It's tough to make telephone calls, only to be met with hostile and rude people on the other end.

It's discouraging to set goals, schedule interviews, explain the technical aspects and benefits of the products and services you provide, overcome customer's objections and misconceptions, and go out of your way to give exceptional service, only to have your customer go elsewhere because they found the same product or service for a few dollars less.

Enough of these experiences can be discouraging for anyone. And after a while, some people just quit trying. But if you keep up the quality of your service to your clients and customers, they will more and more continue to do business with you because that kind of personal service is very hard to find. In the end, it is what makes the difference between the successful and unsuccessful business.

Personal Qualities for Success

Service is essential, but there are also a number of other personal qualities, traits and abilities that, if developed, will help you to become a successful business person and create a successful business.

Sacrifice and Determination

You must determine the price you'll have to pay to be successful. For everything in life, there is a price. And it must be paid before you can realise the rewards. In many instances, it takes sacrifice. I'll tell you a story to illustrate the moral.

A few years ago, in an effort to get a little exercise, one of my friends bought himself a bicycle. He had fun for awhile, but one day a group of experienced riders flew by him on their fast and high-priced racing bikes.

Always a competitive person, my friend decided that he would try to catch them and ride with them. But, try as he might, it was to no avail. They soon disappeared in the distance. This happened a couple of more times and my friend could never keep up, however hard he pedalled. That ate on him and it wasn't long before he found himself back in the bike shop getting the specifications and price for a fast, sleek, high-priced bike.

$2,500 later, he was back on the road just waiting for those riders to catch him so he could ride with them. Not only did he have his new 20 speed racer, but he was completely decked out in cycling shorts and jersey, helmet, and special shoes.

Eventually it happened. The group of riders came up on my friend from behind, and he pumped hard, driving himself to keep up with them. But a quarter of a mile later, breathless and done in, he was "off the back." Soon the riders were gone again, and that really irritated my friend.

But he didn't quit. He bought several books on bike riding, obtained some video tapes, and sought out the help of a neighbour who was a pretty good rider. He worked hard trying to develop his cycling abilities. He rode every morning from 4:30 to 7:30, while his family was still asleep.

He rode in the rain and cold weather, he rode in the heat. He even hired a cycling coach to help him develop his skills. Eventually he entered a local race and, to his surprise, he won! This encouraged him, so he entered another race. Then another. And another. And he kept winning.

MURRAY PRIESTLEY

Now, with the new skills and confidence he was developing, he entered the state and national championships, and placed very high in both. The riders who used to pass him were now coming to him for help and advice. They wondered how he could consistently beat them when he hadn't been riding for nearly as long as they had.

What they didn't understand was that it wasn't how long my friend had been training, as much as what he had put into his training. It wasn't what he did during the race that counted as much as it was what he did during the long, lonely, solitary hours of training.

It was the sacrifices he made, and his determination to be the best, that made the difference between being a social rider or the national champion that he eventually became.

The same concept of sacrifice applies to operating a successful business. If you want to reap the great and abundant rewards your business can provide, you're going to have to do some not-so-glamorous things at some not-so-convenient times.

You are going to have to do what Earl Nightingale said. You are going to have to do "...the things that unsuccessful business owners don't want to do."

That may mean, depending on the type of business you have or operate, that you'll have to leave the comfort of your store or office to visit with people about their needs in their homes or businesses at inconvenient times.

If you have a family, this may prove to be a hardship on you, but if you are just starting out in business, or want to increase your existing business or achieve some new goals, you may have to make that sacrifice. It is important to be sure that you have the support of your family as they will be making sacrifices as well.

If you are not willing to make the necessary sacrifices, then you can't expect to be as successful in business as someone who is willing to make those sacrifices.

Self Responsibility

You are totally responsible for the success of your business and your life. There are no excuses. There may be setbacks or economic downturns, or problems that affect your and your business. Your family situation may change, your suppliers or vendors may discontinue making or providing your favourite products or services, they may change the way they do business with you or even merge with another company. Economies change, corporate policies change, and prospects don't buy from you, and the weather is too hot or too cold.

While those things definitely have an impact on the way you do business and the sales you make, it is important to realise that those things are beyond your control, and it's up to you, and you alone, to accept responsibility for the success of your business.

No matter how bad you might have it, no matter what difficulties or challenges you might encounter, let me assure you that there are many people who have had difficulties and challenges far greater than any you are ever likely to encounter, and somehow, they manage to pull through. And you can do the same.

Here's a little credo that can help you. It contains just ten, two-letter words:

"If it is to be, it is up to me."

That simple one-line sentence says it all. It places the responsibility exactly where it should be... directly on your shoulders.

Commitment

Make a total commitment to your success. Once you have made the decision to be in business, be in that business. Get into it with both feet. Don't let anything hold you back.

Even more than getting into the business; see that the business gets into you. Make a commitment that you are going to succeed, no matter what. And focus on that one business. Don't try to work two different jobs or projects at one time. You can't do either of them justice, and you'll likely end up frustrated and broke, and never know whether or not you could have been successful. Set your goals and then keep yourself moving toward them

Going the Extra Mile

Another personal quality necessary to achieve outstanding success in business is that you must be willing to go the extra mile. It's the "Under promise, over deliver" concept, and can be summed up in the following statement:

"If you are always willing to do more than what you get paid for, the day will come when you will be paid for more than what you actually do."

Robert Cialdini, in his book, "Influence: The Psychology of Persuasion," discusses what he calls the Law of Reciprocity. Basically, it says that when you do something for someone else there's an unstated obligation for them to want to do something for you in return.

So, when you go the extra mile for your customers or clients, you've just set the stage for that law to take effect. But it's only on that "extra mile" that this works. When you give what might be considered "normal" service, or "adequate" service, or even "good" service, you haven't earned the right to expect that law to work for you.

In fact, even performing "knock-out" service often isn't enough to gain you an advantage. We've all come to expect that from any number of businesses.

You've really got to do something special in order to gain an advantage in today's highly competitive marketplace. Then, and only then, can you expect to create that compelling desire in your customer to want to reciprocate.

This simple truth says it all:

"There's no traffic jam on the extra mile."

Time Management

Your time is precious and it is important that you master and take control of your time. Time is a finite commodity. Each one of us has the same 24 hours in each day. When those hours are gone, they cannot be replaced. They are gone forever, never to be recaptured.

You must treat your time as precious, and guard it wisely and selfishly. Don't let anyone disrupt you or take you away from the focus you have on your goals.

People who don't have goals are used by people who do. If you let others draw you away from your goals, you are simply saying that their goals are more important than your own.

If you are serious about business success—really serious, then this is one of the most important and critical areas to defend.

Solutions through Ideas- Increasing Your Effectiveness

Your role as a business owner is to solve your customers' problems. Your ability to determine what your clients want and provide them solutions is a large part of your success. Part of getting you into your best business shape is increasing your effectiveness in coming up with good ideas on how to solve your client's problems in a unique way.

For example, I have a friend who has a software company that sells engineering software to government agencies and educational institutions.

The software is very expensive and the sales process takes a long time, in many cases it will take his salesmen years to get through all the bureaucracy and close the sale. He had continual cash flow problems as a result. A few years ago, he wanted to develop some smaller products and services that he could market to the same clientele that didn't have to take the endless route of approval through all the tiers of the accounting systems in the large institutions. The solution came to him one day when he was at one of his client's offices.

The client showed him some plans to one of the old buildings on campus to help him explain a problem the university faced. The plans were worn and damaged on the edges and even though the client treated them very delicately, even the latest copies were clearly disintegrating.

The University was in the process of having the plans converted over to a CAD program so that they could use them for a remodel they were planning for the building. The problem with the plans, was that some sections were faded or simply unclear, and it took a professional architect or engineer to read the plans and draw them into a CAD program. It was costing them hundreds of dollars just to have each sheet of the plans converted.

In addition, they had a whole room of plans that were in the same state and even though they wanted to preserve them, they couldn't afford it. It occurred to my friend that nearly every one of his clients had the same issue. He had just returned from a conference overseas where a colleague had approached him about a partnership. The colleague had many architects and engineers that needed work. After ironing out the details, my friend started a plan conversion service that used overseas architects and engineers to enter the old drawings into CAD at a price his clients could afford for their archived drawings. He had a built in clientele, a head start on any competition, and his cash flow problems disappeared virtually overnight.

The point is that my friend knew his market, he knew what his company could do, he had peers and colleagues in the industry and there was no one better suited to put all his resources together to solve the problems he was encountering in his business. As the business owner and CEO, you are the solution. Like my friend experienced, your client's problems are just lying around waiting to be seen, you just need to be receptive to those problems and creative about the solutions.

For both you and your customer, things are changing faster than ever before. Technology has become more sophisticated, competition more keen, and consumers––the people who buy your products and services—have become more educated and aware. You are in the unique situation to stay current on the latest technologies for your industry and use them in ways that show your customers that you can apply the latest technologies to solve their problems.

In addition, because your client's choices are ever expanding, regardless of the industry you are in it is very difficult to be either unique, or less expensive. What is important is the service your client receives from everyone in your business. From the receptionist at the front desk to the accounting clerk in the office, everyone who talks to a client must provide them exceptional service and professionalism.   You can be the very best at attracting clients and even selling to them, but what will ultimately make the difference between success and failure is your service.

If you're really going to be effective and successful in the marketplace today, it is necessary, even vital, that you continually change, improve, adjust and update your selling, service, and problem-solving skills, as well as your methods of marketing and general business operation. Keep in mind that:

> "People don't care how much you know,
> until they know how much you care."

One of the best and most effective ways you can show your prospects and customers you care is by helping them solve their problems in a satisfactory, cost-effective, and professional manner.

Getting New Ideas

Since having ideas and recognising opportunities is so crucial to your business. You need to do everything possible to heighten your awareness in this area. You also need to be able to use your knowledge of your customers and their needs, your industry and the new advances in your industry to come up with ideas for products and services for your business. For example, this book is filled with ideas. Yet, how many do you think you will remember once you've closed the cover? Being exposed to a new idea is one thing, but what you do with it once you have it is just as important as getting it in the first place.

Studies on retention show that you remember:

10% of what you read,

22% of what you hear,

37% of what you see,

56% of what you see and hear, and up to

86% of what you see, hear and do.

So an idea that is heard but not acted on is only half as likely to be retained as an idea that is actually put into practice. With that concept in mind then, it is important to understand that if the information presented in this book is to be of any real value to you, it must not only be read, it must be applied. That is to say, it must be experienced, or acted on. And that means it's going to take some effort on your part.

In their book, The Knowing-Doing Gap, authors, Jeffrey Pheffer and Robert L. Sutton mention that every year there are 1,700 new business books published, $60 billion spent on training, $43 billion spent on consultants, and our universities turn out 80,000 graduates with MBA's. Yet, most businesses continue to operate day in and day out in much the same ways as they have always done.

Again, and this theme will keep coming up because it is so important, knowledge without action is no better than no knowledge at all. Just knowing isn't enough. You've got to do something with what you to know.

The ideas presented in this manual work. They're not theory. They're not speculation on what "should" work. And they're not philosophical musings. These ideas, concepts and techniques are currently in use by business owners across the country in one form or another. They're being proven in actual field use day in and day out.

They work for others, and they can work for you. You are going to have to take the time to study them, understand them, and make the necessary modifications to tailor them to your own personal and business style and operation. And then finally, you're going to have to apply them in your business.

Five Steps of Learning and Retention

These five steps will help you to get, use, and keep good ideas. Learning is the acquisition of new information or knowledge, and retention is the ability to capture that information and recall it when wanted or needed. This can be broken down into five steps.

- Impact
- Repetition
- Utilisation
- Internalisation
- Reinforcement

Impact

First, is Impact. That is the receiving of the idea into your mind. Impact can be in the form of a word, a visual observation or a concept. It may involve new information, or it may be a new juxtaposition of old information. This mental processing results in a new concept of the world, however small that concept may be. Thousands and thousands of bits of information, loose ideas, and more fully formed concepts continually wash through the mind. Separating out the useful is the first step; it is all too easily swept away in the torrent of everyday thought. Retention is now the more important facility.

Repetition

To achieve that, the second step is Repetition. One university study revealed that an idea that was read or heard only one time was 66% forgotten within 24 hours. But if that same idea was read or heard repeatedly for eight days, up to 90% of it could be retained at the end.

So once you've read this manual all the way through, go back and read it again. But this time read with a highlighter, a pencil and notepad handy. Mark up the book. Write down the ideas you feel fit your personal business situation. This repetition will help you retain more of the information than if you had read it only once.

Utilisation

The third step in the learning and retention process is Utilisation. This is the "doing" step. It is here that neuromuscular pathways are actually developed, creating a "mindmuscle memory." And according to the study quoted earlier, once you physically experience an action, it becomes twice as easy to recall than if you had heard it only.

Internalisation

Fourth, is Internalisation. That is to actually make the idea a part of you. That may involve some customising or tailoring of the idea to fit your situation or style, but it is vitally important for you to personalise the idea and make it "yours."

Reinforcement

The fifth step is Reinforcement. In order to maximise the effectiveness of an idea, you should continually be looking for ways to support and strengthen it. The more you can support the idea, the more you will believe it, the longer you will retain it, and the more effective it will become in helping you serve your customers' needs.

Now, what does all this have to do with your business? Simply, this. In your daily business and personal activities, as well as throughout your experience with the information presented in this book, you are going to be exposed to a great number of ideas. Some will be brand new, that is, you've never heard them before. Some will be ideas you have heard in the past, but have forgotten. And others will be ideas you come up with on your own as a result of something that was triggered in your mind as you read. Understanding and applying these five steps in the learning and retention process can help you retain more of what you read and experience.

Take Action Exercises

Exercise 5 – What are you worth?

This is a great exercise to help you to understand your position as a business earner, and make sure your basic approach is right. So, what are you really worth? Presumably you have a salary today, and hopefully you earn a reasonable amount of money. However, whatever your annual income, I am going to assume that you would like to earn more. And the sooner, the better. The big question is: how much? Perhaps in five years' time you would like to be making $500,000, or even a million, or possibly two.

Whatever the amount; write it down, and then get your calculator out and divide that number by 1200. When you divide it by 1200 it will show you an approximately hourly rate for what you think you are worth.

Why 1200? Essentially, there is about 1200 productive hours in a year. There are obviously a lot more working hours in a year than that, but not productive. Assume first that you work a five day week. Then you must deduct annual holidays and potential sick leave. More importantly, only a few hours of that eight-hour day are productive. Maybe it is only two hours a day, maybe it is four hours a day. So I am being reasonably conservative when I say that 1200 is how many hours a year that I would expect you to be relatively productive. So if you selected $500,000 as your desired yearly income, then you should come up with a number $416.67 per hour. That is how much money you need to be earning every productive hour for you to earn half a million dollars a year. That is what you believe you are worth.

Why do we do that exercise? If you do work that somebody else could do for less than $416.67 an hour, you are not making the most of your time. Let us say that you do 10 hours work a week that somebody else would do for $20 an hour. You are loosing $397.33 every hour that you do that work yourself. The point is, if you are really worth over $400 an hour, your business will be far better off financially if you get that work done by a person or company that charges less than that.

The caveat is: if you offload half of your work and then sit around the whole day, all you have done is spent money. You have not earned anything more. However, if instead you concentrate on activities that would generate more money, then you will be on your way to earning your half a million or more dollars per year.

Exercise 6 – Solitary Confinement

Try a set-aside two hours per week, where you find a room, away from work, telephones, any and all distractions. No laptop, no mobile phone, nothing but a pad and pen.

Take the time to think. Write your ideas down. Make plans. Decide to take action.

Do this every week. You might find it energising.

4

Part II Shaping Up Your Business.

BECOMING aware of how your behaviour and abilities directly affect your business can be enlightening. You are now painfully conscious that issues and problems in your business can be reflecting your own deficiencies in knowledge and skills. This knowledge may be disturbing, but it is also empowering. It is up to you to enact positive changes and lead your business to success.

Your position as an owner or CEO, can be compared to the captain at the helm of a ship. Despite the currents, winds, storms and calms, you must steer your business to your destination. Mistakes in direction that are not regularly corrected and revised doom your voyage to sure destruction on treacherous reefs, or stagnation in the doldrums. And yes, it is your responsibility. You must keep your eye forever on the horizon. Avoiding disaster relies on your ability to correctly interpret and predict changing market conditions. Simultaneously, you must anticipate other factors which can lead you to disaster. If you are burying yourself in the daily grind of business, your eyes cannot be on the path ahead.

Lifting your eyes from the clutter and work on your desk and looking ahead means that you will be ready for the future when it comes. Gazing into the future requires maneuvering into the best position to reach your goals. A natural result to looking ahead is planning for different business scenarios. You will be designing back up and contingency plans so that you are prepared for change and your business expects the unexpected. You will be steering toward success, not heading for failure.

Strategy

What is strategy? Thinking strategically means looking ahead and concentrating on the long-term. It involves first understanding your vision. Then implementing plans for accomplishing your vision. Most businesses do not think strategically.

The diagram illustrates this concept.

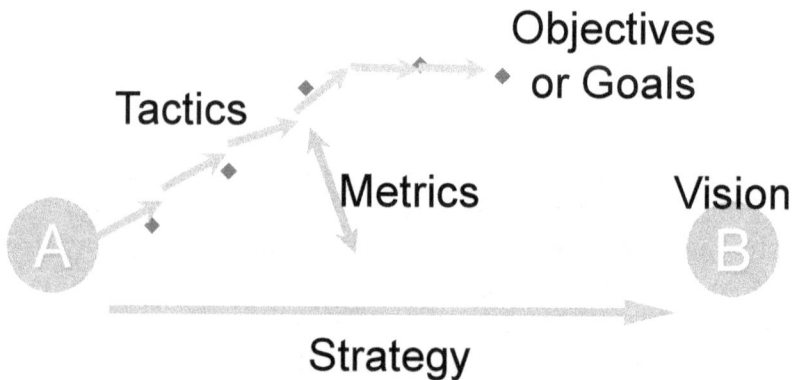

Consider A as where you are now and B as your vision, or the way you want to go. Your strategy includes the overall concept of what you want to achieve and how you generally plan to accomplish it. The actual day to day methods you employ to reach your goals are **tactics**.

For example, if you decide to start an online marketing program this year to increase your sales. That is your strategy. Choosing to use Google Adwords to implement your online marketing campaign would be a tactic. You can use a number of different tactics to achieve the same strategic ends.

Many businesses fail to think strategically, but are mired in tactics. They are forever focused on putting out daily spot fires and are blind to the wider conflagration which is threatening to engulf them. They say: "What are we facing right now? What is that situation right now? Okay, let's go and fix it." They may be very good at dealing with spot fires, but the greater forest is left to burn. A business that constantly expends its resources on dealing with these daily crises cannot move forward, or react to change quickly.

Thinking strategically is about evaluating tactics and their contribution to the overall strategy for your business. You may consider an opportunity, but set it aside because it does not keep your company moving toward your long term goal. You may reconsider that opportunity at another time when it may contribute to your long-range strategy. Businesses which think strategically have a much greater chance of growing and becoming more profitable.

Strategic vs. Magical Thinking

To understand strategic thinking thoroughly, it can be contrasted to a concept called Magical Thinking. The practice of Magical Thinking involves relating certain results to causes that may not necessarily be interconnected. For example, you may know an athlete that has a routine they perform before starting a race or going to a game. They may wear their "lucky socks" or turn around three times fast before approaching the starting block. The athletes associate these behaviors with performing well in their sport. The unrelated behavior has nothing to do with the ultimate task. The ritual however, builds confidence in the athlete which may have a very real affect on the athlete's performance.

Magical Thinking may build confidence for a performance, but has no place in business management. This same thinking translated to the business world can lead to failure. It means deciding on an action, and committing funds to a certain direction rather capriciously. Magical thinking in business involves taking only a cursory glance at the situation and proceeding to make long–range decisions. You can take this casual approach when addressing day-to-day tactics, however it has no place in strategic planning.

Strategic Planning	**Magical Thinking**
Disciplined Approach	"We'll figure it out"
Market Opportunism	"Look at the value"
Real Business Planning	Vision Drive-By
Gory Details	Broad Strokes
Market Focus	Products/Technology Focus
Deep Understanding	Shallow Understanding
Focus on SWOT	Focus on Hype
Focused Execution	"Chasing Rainbows"
Must Move "Thoughtfully"	Must Move Quickly"
Focus on How	Focus on What

Markets

To set your long range focus for your business, you must fully understand your customer base. You should know:

- Who are your customers?
- What are their needs and wants?
- What are their problems?
- Can you solve their problems?
- How much is a solution worth to them?
- Are they willing to pay for a solution to their problem?

One of the ways to discover the answers to these important questions is simply to ask your customers. As obvious as this may sound, many businesses do not ask their customers about their problems. There are many very effective and discreet ways of obtaining this information. For instance, if you own a retail store, talk to the customers. Ask them what you can do for them and listen to what they tell you.

Never bombard customers with lots of questions. Restrict your questions to just a few. Don't go the route of the Commonwealth Bank. This company recently sent me a ninety question survey. I have no intention of answering ninety questions. If they had asked me three questions, chances are I would have provided the answers, and so would most people.

One approach which has proven successful at obtaining customer preferences is to ask two questions a month. Customers usually respond well and are even happy that you are so interested in their needs.

I don't find focus groups too useful. Larger companies sometimes like them, and they are often recommended

by market research companies. My caveat is that they
seldom come up with anything new. When designed
to test a particular product, focus groups are useful.
Otherwise, in my opinion, they produce very little useful
information.

Positioning

The concept of positioning your business is about how
your market perceives your business and your products.
Are you perceived as an expert in your field? Are you
a low cost leader? Do you have niche appeal? You
can position yourself to be anything you really want.
Planning your business's position involves considering
issues such as:

Competition
How is your business perceived compared to others?

Market
How do you address the problems and needs of your
target market?

Uniqueness
What makes you different, or better, or unique in your
field?

Positioning your business is especially important in
fiercely competitive, or crowded markets. Differentiating
your business from the crowd becomes crucial.

To plan your position, first determine where you want
your business to fit in your industry in the broad scheme
of things. One strategy can lead you in a completely
different direction than another. As you follow each
positioning strategy through you need to consider the
qualities of your business and products and what price

category you want to occupy.

Next, tailor and fine tune your position. Identify any specific benefits your business or products offer your customers. These could be such qualities as reliability, safety, convenience, ease of use, etc. You can even choose two benefits and have a primary and secondary position.

Positioning Statement

To communicate your position, you need to develop a positioning statement. Properly developed, it should state in a single sentence or a few words the entire position for your business. This basic idea should exactly fit your business products and services. It should accurately reflect the needs of your customers and target your audience. A very direct relationship exists between choosing your position and communicating this position to your market and the success of your message. For example, don't position your products and services to meet the needs of a high end market if your products are actually more appropriate for a lower end audience. In addition, once established, your company message should not change. You will be using it for your marketing messages, the design of your facilities, your web site and all your promotional materials. Choose your correct position carefully in the start and stay with it.

Business Identity

When creating the position for your business, you need to establish the identity or culture for your business. Your business culture combines your company's vision, mission and position into a cohesive whole. Your culture should communicate everything about your company in your image and style.

Company Vision Statements

The story for your business or your vision statement guides your image and your contribution to society. This story is designed to evoke specific attitudes and images about your business in an emotional way. A great vision statement will enable your customers to understand exactly why you are in business and what you bring to the community. It should outline what you wish to accomplish with your business as well as your plans for contributing to and improving your market.

A very effective vision statement uses a story. It effectively communicates an identity and a history for your business in a unique and friendly manner. To create a story for your business, consider your actual facts. Did you have a dream that you made a reality? Do you have any specific training, experience, or background that you can incorporate as part of your story? Maybe you have a unique history or your business was handed down through your family from your great-grandfather to your grandfather, to your father then to you. Any of these make great stories. They appeal to customers, and build automatic relationships and trust. Customers identify with you and feel they already "know" you and your business.

Stories also have an educational factor. Clients like to be educated. They want to understand as much as possible about what they buy and from whom they buy it. This applies to every industry and every business. So, if you have a story, be sure to tell it. Make sure that your employees understand and can repeat it. If your story is less than compelling, look for ways to enhance it and build it into a better story. But develop your own unique history and company story.

Use Industry Statistics

When developing your company's position you can use a number of methods and resources. One very useful method when finding your approach is to find your "Stadium Pitch." The concept of a stadium pitch is described in a book called *The Ultimate Sales Machine* by Chet Holmes. The Stadium Pitch postulates the idea that an entire stadium, let's say the Telstra Dome in Sydney, is filled with 80,000 potential clients or customers for your business. You are led to the centre of the field, given a microphone, and told you can say anything you want to turn them into buyers of your products or services. A daunting task for many, but what would you say? What would be the first thing that comes out of your mouth?

Here is how I think most people would start. "Hello my name is Fred Smith, and I am very pleased to be here. I just want to welcome you to the stadium. Blah, blah, blah, blah…" By this point you have spoken for 30 seconds and have said nothing of interest to your potential clients. Everyone is already completely bored and half of the people are getting up to walk out. What can you say that will keep the people in their seats? An effective way of immediately gaining people's interest is to tell them something that they did not know. Remember, these people already have something in common with you. They are potential clients.

What if you told them, for example, some of your industry's statistics? Let's say you are in financial planning. You walk to the microphone and you say: "Did you know that in the next twenty years, seven out of ten people sitting in this stadium will retire with less than fifty thousand dollars in the bank?" If you were in the audience, what would you do? Would you leave at this point, or would sit there and wonder, "Wow, that is an interesting statistic. It is not very encouraging but it is interesting." Would you want to hear more? Of course you would. Now you have your audience's interest. You can then add, "for those seven out of ten people, there are five things that they can do over the next month to help ensure they have more than fifty thousand dollars in the bank. Number one, blah, blah, blah, blah. Number two, blah, blah, blah, blah. For more information and a free report on these five plus another five, call 1800 and blah, blah, blah, blah, and you are done.

Taking this approach, you have spoken for maybe five minutes, and have kept everyone firmly riveted to their seats. At the same time, you have likely interested many of your potential clients to ring your number. When they do, you will need to obtain their phone number and other contact details, to send them the reports. You have suddenly increased your mailing list of people interested in your products and services. From this list, you will very likely convert many of these leads to actual clients.

Whether it is a core story or industry statistics, if you have something interesting to say about your business, it is much easier to get and keep the attention of a potential client.

Become An Expert

Another position for your business in the market is to become an expert. Becoming an expert is deceptively easy; you simply declare yourself as one. You may feel this approach is unethical but consider, in your own business, you probably are an expert. As an expert, potential clients and customers look up to you and regard your word as authoritative. When gaining confidence this way, you consequently must back it up with your genuine knowledge and expertise in a field. Positioning yourself and your company as expert in your industry will generate more clients and more revenue.

To increase your standing as an expert there are several methods you can employ.

Publicity
Use press releases to attract the interest of news radio, television, magazines, and newspapers. Being billed as an expert by these media venues will help you gain notoriety as an expert in your field.

Author A Book
Writing a book used to be more difficult. You don't have to be picked up by a large publishing house to be an author. You can self-publish a book quite inexpensively and use it as a marketing and promotional tool.

Let us assume as an example that you want to write a book about ten ways to increase your superannuation. A book on this subject of approximately a hundred or so pages can be both informative and entertaining. All you need to do is provide basic information such as an outline or some notes and have a ghost writer write it. You can have the entire book edited, formatted and printed by professionals so that you end up with a high quality publication based on your concepts and ideas. It is amazing the amount of credibility that you get as a published author.

Another way to use a self-published book is as a giveaway in your store. This concept works regardless of the type of store or business. For example, if you have a fashion store, you can write a book about fashion. For a beauty salon, you can write about improving your image. For a mortgage broker, you can write about getting the best loan. Having the book for sale at your business can be an effective marketing tool, or you can give it away to clients. When potential clients see that you are the author, they will treat you with respect and buy from you with trust.

In addition, books have an element of longevity. If you send out a free report, no matter how nicely presented on A4 paper, it will likely end up in the dust bin in a matter of days. A book stays around in people's homes much longer. People pass them around and may give them away, but they are less likely to be thrown away. Also, books are surprisingly affordable and inexpensive to produce.

The Customer Perspective

When you are working in your business, your focus is most likely head down, with an emphasis on getting work done as quickly as possible. You concentrate your efforts on making your business run efficiently. An efficiently running business does not necessarily mean that your customer is getting the experience you originally intended. . In fact, your business may even have a poor appearance from your customer's point of view. One method that I often recommend to businesses that I assist in becoming more profitable is to pretend to be one of your customers. Look at your business from their view point. What do your customers see, hear and smell? How is your customer treated? Does your customer handling procedures and processes make sense? Are your employees and your environment consistent? Does your business have the look you intended? If you have restrooms, do they fit with the rest of your business and are they clean? Taking your customer's perspective can

THE GREAT BUSINESS SHAPE UP

be eye-opening.

Let us assume that you have a customer support area, where people call an 1800 number for assistance. Call that number, pretend to be a customer and see what happens. You could get a rude shock. Your staff might be well trained, they may even have systems and procedures that they accurately follow. Their attitude toward customers over the phone may not be courteous or appropriate. Even though some employees really enjoy working with customers, the majority do not. Often, employees with incomplete or improper training and monitoring will perform almost any work rather than deal with customers. They may even create projects in order to interact less with customers. This avoidance of customer support and service is surprisingly common.

Examine your business and client interface for an entire day. What would change about your business if you were that client? You can also ask your clients this question. Ask them: "If you could change something about the way we serve you, what would it be?" Listen carefully. Do not become defensive, or argumentative. Treat their comments as valid and important even if they say something that offends or shocks you. Take notes, clarify points you don't understand and thank them warmly when they are done. Take all comments under serious consideration. Implement any changes which will address your customers needs and wants and improve your business in their eyes.

Planning

The planning process is hugely important. The output of your planning is less important. What do I mean by that? Taking time to plan your business activities, then writing it down can be regarded as just a method of focusing your thinking. In fact, the actual document you produce will be obsolete relatively quickly. Situations, circumstances, customers, and your market are all constantly changing. Therefore, planning is an ongoing process which you should consider monthly. Even if you don't take the time to commit your thoughts to any sort of written document, you need to regularly and consistently think about where you are heading in your business.

Writing down your plans helps you focus. Word processing software such as Microsoft Word however is not a good choice for writing business or strategic plans. Use a program designed to condense your thoughts into important points. A program such as Microsoft PowerPoint can help you communicate your ideas quickly and easily, minimise text, keep to the key bullet points and focus on your important ideas I provide a downloadable template for a sample business plan at my site.

Despite the problems of written business plans quickly becoming obsolete, writing a more detailed business plan at set intervals is sound strategy. Depending upon the size of your business, you may also need operational or customer support plans. A regular business plan addresses your vision, and the implementation strategy for your ideas. Be sure to communicate your plans to your staff and encourage feedback. All ideas should be welcomed including negative comments and criticism. You need to fully explore an idea and all its implications in order to come up with the most thoughtful strategy.

Exit Strategy

Another important strategy which most businesses often fail to consider is an exit strategy. This is your long term goal for the "end" of your business.

> Do you intend to retire from your business?
> Are you planning on selling your business?
> Do you want to hand the business down to your son or other family member?
> Are you going to just close the doors and walk away?

Smart business people determine their exit strategy early. In many cases, they design their business to fulfill their exit strategy. This may seem like a backward approach, but this focus actually affects the design of your business. For example, if you start your business with the intent of selling it in three years, would you build your business differently? Would you run it differently? The answer is obviously, yes. The strategies you implement will be heavily influenced by your long term plan. Your goal will be to maximise the value of your business in every way possible.

If a business owner plans their business with the thought of retiring, they will realise the best price possible when they sell. However, according to statistics from Bird Cameron, a well known accounting firm in Australia, a majority of businesses do not have succession plans in place. They have no plan for the sudden loss of the owner, no instructions for a right-hand man to take over the reigns of the company, and no proper plan to sell the business. That is a huge mistake if you want to build the value of your business. You need a right hand person trained as your replacement in cases of emergency or as part of your exit strategy.

The Bird Cameron study also showed that, when business owners reach the end of the lifespan of their business, 30% of business owners simply shut the door and walk away. That means any value that was in the business is lost. Their business gave them a job with a salary. It paid the bills and provided for their family. However, they did not consider the business worthy of selling to somebody else. In many cases, they are probably right. Over the years, they haven't bothered to maximise the potential of their business so that it is a saleable item when they decide to leave.

Most people don't adhere to this philosophy in any other area of their life. For example, if you think of your business as a vehicle, what would you like to be driving? Would you like to be driving a beaten up Nissan Pulsar or a snappy Porsche? Does it make sense to regard your company as an old car that you will junk when you are finished with it? Instead shouldn't you be working to appreciate your asset so that you end up with a top of the range business vehicle that you can sell? An exit strategy encompasses a plan to build your business as much as you can so that it is attractive to somebody else when you want to leave.

Part of a good exit strategy assumes that you have a business that is worthwhile to sell. That means your exit strategy should be closely interlocked with your overall business plan. In addition, that plan must be one that builds value in your business.

Investment Banking World

If your exit strategy includes plans for selling your business, you may want to reach this goal sooner rather than later. This often requires funding from outside sources to quickly maximise the potential for your business. One way of accessing additional funds is to attract investors. These are people who invest money in other people's ideas. There are very specific formats which are considered acceptable to most investors. Approaching investors properly means being prepared. You cannot just arrange a meeting, show up with some promotional materials for your business in hand and expect to come away with enough money for your purposes. Investors look for opportunities which have the best potential for success. They primarily look for the following criteria:

> A great management team
> A great business concept
> A dynamic growing industry

Only having one or two of these elements will seriously handicap you when seeking financial backing. Of these essentials, the most important is being in the right industry. If your industry is going places and you have the other two elements in place, you will have people falling over themselves to be an investor. Even if you have a top notch management team and a solid business idea, if you are in an undesirable industry, you may have to struggle to find backers.

Before they put money on the table, the investment world will ask some specific questions. They will want to know:

- Your objective for your business?
- Is it obvious what you have to do to achieve your objective?
- Where is the real value in the business?

In answer to the value question, you will need to show the areas of your business which indicate what the investor is "buying." You will need to identify beforehand which elements of your business hold the most value. Is the value for your business:

- In the process?
- In the intellectual capital?
- In the customer base?

Once you determine where you value is located, you need to address some additional questions:

- Where is the leverage to capture that value?
- What can you do to multiply that value quickly? (For instance, if the leverage is in the customer side, can you market more effectively to amplify your customer base and use it as leverage for investment?)
- How was the leverage built?
- How are you going to use leverage and is it something that you know how to do?
- What does the business ultimately own?
- What does the business really earn?
- Does the business have the mechanisms to create value or not?
- Is everything done in-house or is some work out-sourced.
- Are the processes and ideas behind the business able to be franchised? (If not franchised, is the company ultimately scalable?)

It is not necessarily just bricks and mortar and a sound business idea that accounts for the value of a company. Different prospective buyers have various reasons for assessing a certain value to a business. For instance, a great strategy for a small business is to target a market dominated by a big company, and deliver something much better than the big company. If they can capture a significant percentage of the market and annoy the big company enough, the larger company will want to buy them out. For example, this scenario happens a lot in the cosmetic industry. A new product from a small company grabs a slice of the market and the big company has no option but to purchase the smaller company. In such cases, an investor's assessment of the smaller company's value may be much higher than it would be under different circumstances.

One final question from the investment banking world is:

- Can the value that is found in your company easily be converted to cash?

Investors want to know just how they are going to profit from their investment, and so you as the business owner need to be able to figure out how to get to the wallet of your customer. This again requires your unique in-depth knowledge of your business and of your customers' needs and how to best meet them.

Take Action Exercises

1. Develop some ideas for a book that you can use as a promotional item or marketing tool. What topics interest you? What areas of your business would your client like to understand more?

2. Do some research on www.elance.com to see what it might cost you to have someone write your book for you.

3. Complete the One Page Business Plan for your current business using the sample business plan on the following page as a guide.

Sample Business Plan

The key to the one page business plan is to keep it short, sweet and to the point.

① **Vision**	Within the next 3 years, grow CGP into a $3 million national consulting firm specializing in creative leadership development programs for Fortune 1000 companies.
② **Mission**	We help companies develop more leaders!
③ **Objectives**	• Increase revenue to 1.8 million in FY 2007. • Increase gross margin to 54% from 32% by 12/31/07 • Earn a pretax profit of $450,000 for FY 2007. • By 12/31/07, establish a client base of at least 10 companies.
④ **Strategies**	• Leverage CGPs worldwide identity as entree into business consulting. • Build company awareness by networking at executive level. • Create simple, easily-produced materials from existing CGP products. • Use first clients to define product offering/build momentum. • Use a "train the trainer" approach to maximize reach in larger clients. • Create product ranges so that any business can afford a co-creative management system.
⑤ **Plans**	• Develop written marketing plan by 2/16/07. • Trademark "Core Group Process" by 4/4/07. • Publish 4 quarterly newsletters, send the first to 1500 potential clients on 3/15/07.. • Deliver 5 workshops by 6/30, another 4 in Q3, and 3 in Q4 to net 4 new clients • Create high quality company brochure by 7/1/07. • Create series of four mini-books on new personnel management techniques by 12/31/07.

5

Building Massive Value
in your Business

CREATING a successful business with massive value requires making fewer mistakes and better decisions than your competitors. Mistakes in some areas more significantly affect your bottom line than others. When you learn these common mistakes and pitfalls waiting for you in business, you can avoid them. Learning and implementing the successful strategies and techniques that other businesses employ will benefit you as well.

Shape Up Your Marketing

The greatest potential for both success and failure lies in sales and marketing. For this reason, despite the fact that it may not be included in every job description in your company, everyone is responsible for marketing. Through your employee's performance, manners and appearance, everyone affects the bottom line. Why? In nearly every business, sales depend upon repeat customers, word of mouth referral, or expanded purchase of additional products and services. Your business's reputation can spread quickly and everyone contributes to that reputation. People will judge your entire business on their contact with just a few representatives of your company. This means that every single person in your business must be sales conscious!

Another fact that you need to understand as well is that your business is not about what you make or offer as a service. It is actually about **selling** what you make, or **selling** your services!   In fact, every business is primarily a marketing business. For example, you may believe that you manufacture plastic cups as your business. Your primary business shouldn't be seen as producing plastic cups however, but selling plastic cups. When you accept this fact, you can begin to concentrate on that activity, and your business will start to grow.

Now, there are other things that you need to have in your business to make sure you can support your marketing and sales efforts. You need to have systems and processes in place that streamline your ability to sell your products and services and support your customers. Having a cumbersome sales system can handicap your sales. In the end, everything in your business must be focused on finding, getting and keeping customers. Selling and marketing to your clients should be accomplished in the most effective and efficient way possible that makes sense to the customer.

Ten Marketing Mistakes

When designing your marketing strategies, you should learn from the mistakes of others. Errors are costly and whenever you can use tried and proven concepts, you should implement them. In fact, you shouldn't take any chances with your marketing. This is not an area where you want to forge new territory. Stay with the techniques that have worked for other successful businesses. The following are some common mistakes that businesses make when trying to attract customers to their business. You can easily avoid most of them and you will likely have to admit that you've made the mistakes as well. Whether you recognise them or not, learn from them. It will help you avoid any really calamitous marketing disasters.

Mistake #1 - Failure to Test Marketing

The first marketing mistake is not testing your marketing. Brochures, sales-letters, and advertising of all types go out to customers and potential customers everyday that is never tested. If you are unfamiliar with the concept of testing your marketing, you may not even know how to do it. Basically, you need to find the most effective way to reach your clients and potential clients. If you don't compare different approaches, you won't know which is the most successful. For instance, a simple process such as greeting prospective clients when they contact your business can make a huge difference in converting potential clients into customers. That first point of contact needs to be done correctly. It rewards you to test a number of approaches until you discover the most effective and productive one.

Similarly, if you test the headline on a brochure, do you get a better response if you use one headline over another headline? As soon as you find the one that more people read, then use it. There is evidence to suggest that by testing headlines, you can increase experience up to 21 times improvement. This means instead of getting 10 customers, you get 210 customers for the same price. That is an enormous difference that you cannot afford to ignore, so remember, testing is vitally important! A common way to test your advertising headlines is by using a unique phone number in your ad and tracking your response by phone number.

Mistake #2 – Not Using Direct Response Marketing

The second marketing mistake is running institutional advertising instead of direct response advertising. Institutional advertising may look good, show a nice picture, and have a witty slogan, but it does not motivate the reader to do anything. Direct response advertising is designed to elicit a response. It says something like: "Call this number now for a free CD" or "Do this to get this." Direct response advertising also allows you to measure everything you do. For example, if you run a new ad in the newspaper, you can tell exactly how many people call about that ad if a call to action is central to the message. So, use direct response advertising whenever appropriate to avoid wasting your selling opportunities.

Mistake #3 – Not Using Your Unique Selling Proposition

Not including or even mentioning your Unique Selling Proposition is the third marketing mistake. Spending valuable resources to develop just the right USP then not using it is costly. Remember, your USP tells customers and potential customers why they should be dealing with you and gives you an edge over your competitors. So don't keep it a secret. Utilise this important element of your marketing everywhere!

Mistake #4 – Not Expanding Your Services

Number four marketing mistake is a failure to expand your services. You should continuously be looking for ways to give your clients not only what they want, but even more than they expect. In the example of a retail fashion store, if they want to expand their business, they will be looking beyond dresses and accessories. They will explore ways for their existing customers to spend more money with them. They may consider providing something else to buy or a service that gets customers into the store. They could have a fashion parade or a fashion consulting service. Once potential clients are in the store, it is much more likely they will see something they like or the salespeople will be able to interest them in buying. Also, if they charge for the consulting service it is another revenue line to bolster their bottom line.

Mistake #5 – Failing to Address the Real Needs of the Client

The fifth marketing mistake is failing to address the real needs of the client. Do you understand what the client wants? Remember that people buy solutions to their problems. They buy what they need. For example, if a customer buys an expensive new formal gown from a store, they are not buying a dress. They are buying admiration from fellow dinner party attendees. They are buying compliments, or perhaps they are buying motivation to lose the ten pounds they must to fit the dress properly. If you sell and install doors and windows, when your customer buys a front door, they are not just buying a door to keep the weather outside. They may be buying prestige, or trying to keep up with their neighbours. You must always be aware of your customers' underlying needs when they buy your products and services and design your sales efforts to target those needs.

Mistake #6 – Keeping Your Business Problems a Secret

The number six marketing mistake is not letting the clients know that you have some business problem that may be affecting them. Don't keep it a secret. You want more communication, not less. This may go against your better judgement if you are a business owner. But, if you have a problem, tell the customer. In essence you should say: "I am sorry" or "I apologize, we have a problem. Here is what we are doing about it." Most clients will not only readily overlook it, but they will also be pleased that you took the trouble to keep them in the know. The important part of this equation is solving the problem and making sure it does not happen again.

Mistake #7 – Making It Difficult for Your Customers to Buy From You

The seventh marketing mistake is failing to make buying from you as easy as possible for the customer. This is particularly true on websites. How many sites have you visited that are either difficult to navigate or lack the information that should be there? Most frustrating of all is when you actually want to buy, but cannot find how to order and pay. If you finally discover how to order and pay, you may find the site doesn't accept the form of payment you want to use. For example, the site may accept check, or credit card, but not PayPal. Obviously that site is going to lose sales.

In a direct mail business that I own, I accepted credit cards, but did not accept checks. When I added checks to my accepted forms of payment, my sales not only increased, but I began to receive money orders as well. This simple change increased sales by 20%. Instead of one hundred people buying, there were suddenly 120 people buying. These are customers I had been missing until I began to accept checks and money orders.

Mistake #8 – Failure to Inform Customers for Reason Behind Great Deals

Marketing mistake number eight is failing to tell customers why the deal you are offering is legitimate. People are happier if they understand the underlying reason for your pricing. They may want to buy your product, but hesitate because the price is "too low to be real." You need to provide them a proper reason to trust you and believe you are giving them a good deal.

For instance, a going-out-of-business sale may not be a good enough reason. Too many businesses have going-out-of-business sales and are still there two years later. So, provide your customer with the real reason. Why are you going out of business? Are you going out of business at this location so you can move to another location? One great example of telling the reason behind your low prices is given by a furniture store that received heavy damage to its building from a large hail storm. The hail smashed part of the roof and some of their furniture was water damaged. They capitalized on this disaster and held a water damage sale. When they advertised the reason for their sale, hundreds of people came from all over the area to buy their furniture at bargain prices. The water damage incident and sale also increased regular sales dramatically. People had confidence that the prices they were getting were actual bargains.

Mistake #9 – Failure to Stay With Marketing Campaign that is Working

Marketing mistake number nine arises out of number eight. Don't discontinue an effective marketing campaign prematurely. As long as people are still flocking to the store to buy the water damaged furniture, why would you stop the campaign? You need to be very careful, however, with this approach. You should monitor the response you get very carefully and when your sales begin to slow, you should discontinue the campaign immediately. Running the campaign too long can result in loss of confidence in your market. You will be in the same position as the company that runs a going out of business sale, but never goes out of business. Customers will feel deceived and you may have low response to new campaigns that you run.

You need to remember this for all your advertising campaigns. If you have an ad running that requires 20 orders to cover costs, and the first week it generates 100 orders, you should run it again until orders begin to slow. It is only when response to your ad slows down that a new campaign is warranted.

Mistake #10 – Losing Focus for Intended Customer

Lastly, marketing mistake number ten is forgetting to focus on your intended market. If one of your products or services has a wide appeal, you should consider breaking your marketing efforts into smaller segments. By breaking up the larger potential customer demographic into more personalized segments, you can tailor your message to the smaller but still coherent groups within the larger group. This marketing technique is called 'niche' marketing. It takes thoughtful and creative planning, but targeting niche groups rewards your extra efforts with extra profits.

As an example, I have a business that focuses generally on small to medium sized enterprises (SMEs). That is a very broad demographic. Focusing on the entire group as a homogenous unit can be difficult. Instead, I break the market into niche groups. One sub-unit that I target is moms who are trying to start a business from home: Mompreneurs, I call them. I develop my messages to address the unique problems encountered by Mompreneurs so that they feel I understand their particular concerns in business. If my advertising tried to be all things to all people and tried to address every possible area of SME's, I would miss this very exciting market. Mompreneurs would likely feel they were too insignificant to be one of my clients. By targeting their niche precisely, I am more likely to sign them up as clients. I try to do that with all the niche markets that comprise my greater SME customer base.

Growing Your Business

For your business to grow rapidly, your vision must be crystal clear and everybody concerned in your business must be able to easily understand it. They must understand the systems that make it work, and the mechanisms that make it scalable. A business must also operate quickly from day to day in order to grow quickly. You must not be afraid of the speed of development that you may be required to oversee. The operation of a business can be easily compared to the aerodynamic qualities of a moving object. The faster an object moves, the greater the drag that is exerted by the air. Air represents the normal outside influences your business experiences everyday, and drag represents your ability to react to changing market conditions. A high amount of drag does not mean that you are failing in business. However, the more you streamline your business and make it more agile, the less drag holds you back. Streamlining your business and making continuous planning adjustments are the hallmark of successful businesses. Every step to make your business be more responsive to your customers and adjust to changes in your industry should also bring you closer to your core strategy. You must keep your vision and long term goals firmly in sight. Streamlining the day-to-day tactics only enables you to achieve your goals more quickly and easily.

Become Dispensable

Structuring your business for maximum value requires that the business owner or CEO becomes dispensable. Being indispensable hampers your efforts at creating a business which attracts potential investors and buyers. To become dispensable, you need to employ a "right-hand person." This person should coordinate the daily operation of the business leaving you free to oversee the task of building your business. Having a second-in-command enables potential investors to recognise your business as one that will continue to run smoothly even if something happens to you. They will envision your business more as an autonomous entity such as a machine not dependent on any one person. For your business to have maximum value, it must be a valuable commodity with or without you at the helm.

Investors will also view the ability of your business to be profitable. You should consider profit as important not only for yourself, but for potential investors as well. In fact, your company should be structured with profit prioritised. Keeping your customers happy is a must, but ultimately your reason for satisfying customers is to make a profit. Having your business generate profits without you being there results in a more valuable company.

Getting the right person to take over day-to-day operations must be done carefully to avoid the numerous pitfalls which can influence your selection. Consider delegating the task of hiring a second in command to someone you trust, or a staffing expert. There are a number of reasons for not doing this job yourself. First, hiring good employees may not be your strong point. For example, I know my personal limitations and I am not good at hiring staff. Because of this, I recommend using experts to winnow the field of candidates. Another reason arises in the likelihood that you will chose a candidate to whom you relate well. If you are intimately involved in the hiring process for your right-hand person, you may feel most at home with someone very much like you. Your right-hand person should mirror a few of your strengths, but should more importantly, complement your abilities by compensating for some of your weaknesses.

Becoming dispensable should be considered a priority, but it can be done in steps. The first move might be to offload some of what you do to an outside contractor wherever appropriate. It may surprise you what can be contracted out, so keep an open mind about this concept. Evaluate your tasks for areas and specific jobs which can be out-sourced or delegated. There are companies on the Internet that can broker just about any skill you can imagine. You may also want to consider keeping these tasks in-house by training your staff to assume some of your less specialized duties. However you accomplish offloading the work, it should be done by someone else. In addition, the faster you offload the work, the quicker you will be able to concentrate on how to go get more clients and leverage your assets to generate more value in your business.

Building Your Business' Net Worth

What is net worth? This concept can best be explained with a balance sheet. This "net worth" statement provides you with a financial snapshot of your business. It defines the financial soundness of your company at the time of the net worth evaluation. Statements of your net worth can be done any time, but are most commonly set for financial milestones such as the beginning and ending of your accounting period.

To compute net worth you can use the following formula:

Assets - Liabilities = Net Worth

The statement records the value of what you own, or the assets of your business, and the financial claims against those assets, or your liabilities or debts. By comparing your assets against your liabilities, you come up with the net worth of your business. This equity, or the amount that the value of your business exceeds your liabilities, reflects the value of your business and likewise, the extent of your ownership of your business. You would receive this amount upon the sale of your business after collecting all your outstanding accounts and paying all your debts and liabilities.

A fundamental difference exists between a person who works in a wage based, or salaried position and a person who owns a business. Business owners anticipate that their company will grow in net worth. They usually intend to reap the benefits of their increased labour and risk by building equity. The person working in the "security" of a job labours primarily for the amount of money they get every week or every month. They exchange their time for money in a direct ratio. Business owners should also draw a salary. They should be taking a reasonable amount of money out of the business on a regular basis to pay for their normal living expenses. Ultimately, a large number of business owners worry less about their personal expenses, and concentrate on building their business into something that has a high net worth.

Selling Your Business

Let us look at a couple of the statistics related to selling a business. A study by RSM Bird Cameron in 2007, predicted that over the next ten years a very large number of small-medium businesses will be sold. These business sales will result largely from the group of people referred to as the baby boomer generation. The baby boom era produced a generation of people with a high degree of entrepreneurial spirit. For a number of factors they pursued starting their own businesses over corporate employment. So the late 60s, 70s and 80s, saw a higher number of small businesses being started than before. For various reasons the baby boomers wanted to get out of the normal workforce and into the flexible environment of small business ownership.

Now as baby boomers reach retirement age, they are looking to sell their businesses and "cash out". The study from Bird Cameron estimated that 80% of baby boomer business owners have their entire personal net worth tied up in their business and must sell their business in order to retire. Over the next ten years, this statistic will be reflected in the large number of businesses which become available for sale.

As we discussed previously, many business owners, in

fact 33% according to the statistics, have not created an exit strategy for their business. They do not perceive that their business has any value and they intend to simply shut their doors and walk away. These business owners have worked hard to build their business, develop goodwill and customer satisfaction and yet, they do not recognise, or know how to prepare their business for sale.

Preparing a Business for Sale

Unfortunately, 75% of businesses placed on the market never sell. This statistic can be discouraging, but if you properly prepare your business for sale, you can dramatically increase your odds of selling your business and getting the most amount of money for it. First, you need to set your business up to target a certain type of buyer. Let us have a look at that. You need to ask, who is going to buy the business? Most people in the small business world end up selling their business to someone who is actually a staff member of the business, or a competitor. Both of these buyers are going to value your business in a way that does not give you the maximum amount of money. In fact, their goal will be to pay you the least amount of money. Your focus as a seller is to find someone willing to pay you the most amount of money for your business. To find this buyer you need to look outside of your industry to investors rather than buyers who want to work in the business.

To design your business to appeal to investors, it comes back to the concept that your business needs to be able to run without you being there. To illustrate this point, consider a coffee shop where the owner opens the doors every morning and locks the doors every night. As an owner, you come to work, do everything yourself or with the help of a couple of employees, get some money and go home. In this case, only buyers who want to buy a job for themselves will be interested. Remember, these buyers are in the "least amount of money" category.

Your goal, therefore, should be to add value to your business to attract investors. Becoming an "absentee owner" where you own the business but don't actually work in it, will catapult your business to a much higher net worth than other businesses an investor may consider buying. To add equity, you should think of your business as an entity that can function without you. Using the coffee shop example, if you design your business so that your employees can take care of every aspect of your business without you there, you are free to grow your business. You can "feed" your employees ideas; have them execute the ideas; and build your customer base. The coffee and other products are sold without you being directly involved in the day to day activities. This type of business will be worth more money and attract the interest of investors. In an upcoming chapter on systemising your business, you will learn more about streamlining your business to run efficiently without you.

How to Increase the Value of a Business for Sale

In every industry there are metrics or measures called benchmarks that indicate the value of a company. The higher benchmarks you can attain for your business and the more systemized you can be, the larger price you will obtain for your business. Ultimately the multiplier for all businesses is net profit, or EBITA which stands for Earnings Before Interest Tax and Amortization. Usually the benchmark is determined by applying a formula to this number which results in a net profit multiplier. For financial planning businesses, this multiplier can be 2.1 to 2.3 times net profit. For your industry, it might be 1.5 to

1.7. If you improve on the standard benchmarks for your industry, you have a far better chance of getting 3 to 4 times net profit.

For example, one benchmark that investors typically use when they evaluate purchasing a financial planning business is the funds under management. This is the amount of money that the financial planners for that business have and are actively managing. They make a commission on this amount. This is recurring income that the business can use in making forecasts. If you apply the standard multiplier of 2.1 to 2.3 times the funds under management it will give you an idea of what an investor would be prepared to pay for the business.

For the motel industry the benchmark used is the margin or the amount of net profit for a motel. Another benchmark is utilization which indicates the amount of days each year where all of the beds in the motel are full. You can compare these figures to other motels in the same category in order to evaluate the relative position of a motel in the industry.

As a business owner preparing your business for sale, you need to know the benchmarks in your industry. Once you know the standards expected for your industry, you can optimize your business so your metrics are better than average. For example, consider a motel business with a net profit of 15% and utilization of 60%. If these figures are the industry benchmark, you should work to obtain a net margin of 17% and utilization of 70%. This will enable your motel to exceed the performance of other motels in your category. With both of your benchmarks better than average, your evaluation will likely to be many times greater than a business with only average performance. To an investor, this is a financial exercise.

They can look at the numbers and work it out as though you are an investment.

One of the aspects investors consider when making an investment is the risk involved. Depending upon how risk averse the investor is, they will select different investments. They will consider investments based on their own age and how much effort it will take to make a business more profitable. Factored in is how much money they want to invest versus how much money they will make in a few years' time.

An investor might look at our sample motel business with the net margin of 17%. If they invest $100.00, their return at the end of the year will be $117.00. Now, if the utilization is also higher than average, the investor can look and see what else can be done to improve the metrics for the business. With a 17% business, they are starting at a higher income point than one with only a 15% margin. This one factor alone will make your business more attractive to an investor.

Take Action Exercises

1. Go through each of the 10 marketing mistakes and grade yourself. 0 = you are making this mistake and 10 = you are not doing this.

2. What areas can you make an immediate change to?

3. Decide now to build your business as though you were going to sell it.

4. What one area would you need to change in order to immediate improve the value of the business?

5. Make a plan to start implementing this within a week.

6

Execute Better than Anybody

BACK when I first joined the workforce right out of school, I was lucky enough to have a number of mentors. These mentors gave me guidance and frequently led me through "what not to do," an essential element in discovering how to succeed. I have found over the years that these "pearls of wisdom" apply to anything you put your hand to, and applying them in your life will put you on the path to success.

These were the sort of people who give you one or two sentence answers. They never wasted words and their advice always hit the mark. Few words, but meaningful.

One of the "pearls of wisdom" that has stuck with me throughout my career is this:

"Thinking, talking, planning count for nothing – doing counts for everything"

This "pearl of wisdom" may evoke a sense of dissonance and you may be considering that planning and thinking are absolutely important – and they are. But in over 20 years of working with clients and businesses, the fact is that people have an innate desire to avoid their clients and will do more and more things that have less to do with the end client – given almost any excuse. It's just a simple fact that the majority of people do not like to deal with sales or for that matter directly with other people in a business situation.

So yes, thinking and planning, and even talking are important – but by themselves the danger lies in that little or nothing else will happen but the planning. And at the end of the day, it's the doing that gets the work done – which allows you to get paid and to pay your employees and suppliers.

Ultimately, in business, the company that is best at executing and delivering products and services obtains a huge advantage over the competition. Effective marketing and selling can attract customers, but your employees must deliver on what your company promises to retain customers. Proper management of your workforce ensures that your employees are executing the mission of your company and following your systems and procedures. You can plan and design systems to infinity, yet if your employees do not implement them properly the result will be failure.

Based on what I have experienced, here are some factors that contribute to shaping up your business for maximum success – by focusing on doing stuff – executing.

Management Techniques

Most business owners and CEO's have difficulty accomplishing everything that must be done in any given day. Two factors perpetuate and compound this problem.

1. **Trying to do everything yourself**
2. **Trying to do many jobs at once**

Both of these problems can be addressed and the personal execution of the work you really need to do greatly enhanced.

Trying to Do Everything Yourself

This first problem—trying to do everything yourself— can be solved with relative ease. Simply don't do it. Get help. When you try to do everything on your own, you become a bottle neck to productivity and growth for your business. The only way for your company to grow is to expand your staff and outsource some elements of your business process. From your point of view that means delegating tasks which do not require your personal attention. Your time is worth money and when you examine your tasks, you may find that others are not only better suited than you to accomplish a task, but that less expensive people can be utilised resulting in lower costs for your company.

When you want to get something done, evaluate the task on whether or not it can be delegated. If it requires your specific knowledge, determine if you can divide the task into smaller segments which can be delegated while maintaining control of the main project. Perhaps you can train someone, or have them report to you for critical decisions. Examine all of your responsibilities with the goal of reducing your workload and ultimately the costs for your company.

MURRAY PRIESTLEY

Trying to Do Many Jobs at Once

Once you've solved the first problem, the second one—trying to do everything at once—is somewhat ameliorated. Delegating unnecessary tasks should have freed up your time for more productive leadership tasks which are critical to the growth of your company. Now, when addressing the remaining tasks, do not try to multi-task. The brain isn't organized to productively manage tasks in this way and none of your tasks will be done really well or in the most efficient manner. Or at least mine isn't anyway and yes, I'm male, and most of us are like this. Multi-tasking is the equivalent of taking longer to do many jobs poorly.

To minimise multi-tasking and increase your efficiency, focus on one thing at a time. Block time out to do one job and arrange to avoid interruptions. You cannot be answering phone calls, emails and have people knocking on your door and efficiently do anything else.

I can literally get a day's work done in two hours if I just focus on it and get it done. I just set aside a period of time for a specific purpose and presto - it's done. So my advice is - learn to focus. And perhaps more importantly, set aside blocks of time where you are uninterrupted, so you can focus.

My preferred time-management technique is a simplified version of David Allen's "Getting Things Done." this technique involves managing your daily activities and tasks so that you accomplish as much as possible. David Allen's approach emphasises staying abreast of a heavy workload in a "relaxed manner." For more information on his methods, you will find he has free articles and information on his website: http://www.davidco.com.

Focus

When you are able to focus on an activity without interruption you can accomplish far more than you can with constant interruptions. This concept works not only for you, but for your business. You should evaluate your business environment in terms of enabling your staff to focus. Do your work areas maximise concentration and minimise interruptions? If you have a nine to five environment, can your employees start working at 9:00 and work in a concentrated fashion until 5:00 PM? Upon careful examination you may find that your business environment encourages interruptions and reduces productivity in your staff. Your employees may only have a few hours each day that they can actually focus on their work.

To design a more efficient work environment, you need to consider several factors. If you have office workers, do they have a very clear defined desk space where they are able to focus on getting work done? Are there lots of miscellaneous papers and files lying around? These items contribute to drawing attention away from the task at hand. They distract attention from the work. Ideally an absolutely clean desk with nothing on it other than a computer and any files necessary to accomplish a task is best. I have never actually seen such a scenario in real life, but in theory, this uncluttered approach to work is desired. Everyone has their unique style for work, which should be accommodated whenever possible. By providing the appropriate tools and an uncluttered environment where your staff can focus will result in more work being done.

Leadership

When you imagine a strong leader, visions of a bossy
manager or a Draconian dictator may come to mind.
However, being a strong leader does not necessarily
mean ruling with an iron fist. It can mean leading by
example. Providing a model for an efficient worker by
your own example has been proven to be an effective
leadership style. You can demonstrate through your
own actions that getting work done efficiently is
possible. Develop your skills in time management and
implement organisational techniques in your personal
workplace. If somebody requests for you to accomplish
a task, respond quickly. Keep your focus on the vision
for the company, and what you want to achieve in the
future. Avoid becoming bogged down in the daily process
of your business and free your time to lead. Don't "hit
the roof" when something wrong happens, but maintain
your focus on the long term view for your business. This
attitude in a boss fosters a sense of loyalty in your staff.
If you concentrate on your duties and allow your staff
to focus on their tasks, the result will be that the work
is accomplished efficiently and your business operates
smoothly.

Teaming, Partnering and Joint Ventures

If you are the only worker in your business, then your
growth is limited by your capability to produce. In order
for your business to grow, you must find a way to take
on more work. Outsource what you can, or partner with
another company. Team up with others so you can get
more work done. If you have the ability to accomplish
more tasks in the early stages of a business, you will
certainly be in a better position for growth. Many
companies focus their attention on accomplishing work.
They lack skills however, in getting the work.

Hiring

If you are looking to grow your business, then you ultimately must hire staff, independent contractors or consultants. Adding people to your staff means that you need to develop your human resource and management skills. The number one reason why employees fail to integrate well into a business is because of improper hiring practices. Job titles and duties often lack clear definition and description. The person responsible for hiring often fails to consider the attitudes of a potential employee in addition to their skills. Prospective employees must have personality traits and attitudes that are compatible with the work environment. If you hire somebody and they do not work out, then you only have yourself to blame. Whether you are hiring or you have delegated the task, you are primarily responsible for your hiring practices.

Many employers don't consider a hiring method which uses multiple interviews. This technique enables you to evaluate a potential employee on several different occasions. You can watch the response of potential employees and delve past the "first interview" best behaviour façade to the real person beneath. By interviewing many times, you have the opportunity to test reliability, responsiveness and reactions using a series of techniques. You can also have different people in your company interview a candidate. Using this method, a costly inappropriate hire may occur, but the likelihood of this happening is vastly reduced.

Attitude and Skills

Take time to clearly define what kind of person you are seeking for your company. For example, if you are a very small business, you may need someone to be highly resourceful and flexible in their time and duties. In such cases, be sure to communicate that you are looking for someone with flexible hours whose duties will encompass many roles in your business. When evaluating a candidate for a position in your company, consider more than skills. Weigh the attitude of a candidate heavily. What attitude and skills are you seeking in an employee? Defining exactly what you want and need in an employee helps you avoid costly hiring mistakes.

Skills

Let us look at skills first. Skills are the mechanical things. These are knowledge based activities which someone can be trained to perform. For example, knowledge of how to use a PC or Macintosh is a skill. You may also require that a candidate be able to use Microsoft Office software. The position may require that they have a level of knowledge about the work that you want them to do. Consider where you are willing to relax your requirements for a good candidate. Must the candidate be highly proficient in a software program, or would more general knowledge be acceptable?

Do you have an aggressive training program?

Have you systemised a lot of the procedures in your workplace?

As a result of your training and systemisation efforts,

you may be able to hire a lesser skilled worker with good potential at a lower wage. You will still get the work done, but at a less costly price. A candidate's attitude then becomes as important as or even more important than their skills.

Attitude

What is the attitude you desire an employee in your business to have?

Do they need to be flexible?

Do they need to be fun loving?

Should they be able to fit into an environment where everyone enjoys a high degree of camaraderie and goes out together for a drink on Friday night?

Is your environment more formal, with a professional office arrangement?

If you have a team of highly creative employees but lack "detail oriented" people then you may have a balance problem. You could consider hiring an employee based on their ability to take care of details. A "detail" person could free up time for your creative people by structuring the work in a logical fashion. Your creative people can then do what they do best.

There is a great book called "Top Grading" which provides an excellent study on how to evaluate and hire for the attitudes of people. The interviewer must discover the attitudes of a potential candidate. Determining attitudes enables you to assess the ability of a candidate to "fit in" to your work environment and eliminate those who would not appreciate your work climate. Remember, skills can be taught. Attitudes are very difficult if not impossible to adjust.

Part Time and Virtual Staff

Through the power of the Internet, you now have the world at your fingertips. Many staffing options become available through the web in addition to traditional fulltime employees. Obviously, you can hire part-time staff but there is an increasing demand for virtual assistants. These are people that typically live and work at another location. Your communication is often reduced to phone calls or email. However, utilising contractors who work from home or are located in other economic environments can enable you to off load administrative work or work which requires less skilled labour.

This pool of virtual labour consists of many types of people. Some are stay at home parents who can only work 10 or 20 hours a week from home. In many instances, these "part time virtual employees" are highly competent people whose focus on their family removes them from the conventional work force. Tapping into this resource can enable you to hire a top flight employee part time on a contract basis and eliminate the overhead of an onsite employee.

You can also use virtual assistants or companies that live in India, Pakistan, Romania, or almost anywhere around the globe. The current going rate for highly competent well educated labour is around $5.00 to $10.00 an hour. You can off load and systemize some of the work in your business to these individuals or companies and still expect the same competency of work as you would from an onsite employee.

An interesting aspect to using labour in other locations is the time difference. Your virtual assistants may live in countries half way around the world from you which may enable them to accomplish work "overnight."

As an example, I recorded much of the text of this book. Right now, I am talking into a Dictaphone. When I finish for the day I will send my recordings to a transcription company in a different time zone that will convert my recordings into text while I sleep. This makes a very efficient work methodology for me. When I start work in the morning, my recordings from the previous day are transcribed and waiting for me. I simply pick up where I left off and continue on. The use of virtual assistants can vastly increase your productivity in a number of ways and I highly encourage you to consider this resource.

The key to taking advantage of virtual assistants, outsourcing companies or any offsite employee lies in your business systems. Using your systemising techniques be sure that you have instructions well documented for tasks you assign to off site labour. Clearly define everything you want your virtual assistants to accomplish. Be sure to specify the format you require and any other details that are important to ensuring the work is done correctly. The clearer you can be about what you want and how you want it done, and the more systemised your outsourced tasks, the better result you will get.

Rewards and Incentives

As an employer, you encounter all types of people and work ethics. Hire wisely by getting to know your potential employees before you offer them a job, and consider attitude as well as skills. If you do this, you increase your chances of having a work force on which you can rely. A continual issue for many employers is productivity. Many methods have been tried to motivate employees to apply themselves to their jobs and encourage excellence in their work.

One successful technique involves offering rewards and incentives based on outstanding performance by either your company or by an individual. For company based rewards, if certain profit goals or sales targets are reached, or if you land a good contract, the achievement is shared companywide. Everyone in the company should receive a bonus. This sort of incentive generates increased loyalty and a sense of personal responsibility toward the well being of the company by your workforce.

Personal incentives reward individuals for outstanding achievements. If people do what is expected, then they receive their normal wage or salary. If they perform over and above what is expected then you should consider offering incentives to encourage this behaviour. Incentives are an effective reward strategy and contrary to popular belief, most incentives are not cash based.

To find the most effective incentive program for your company, do some research. If you are the owner of the company do not assume what your staff will be motivated by the same incentives that may motivate you. As a business owner, you already think differently from your employees. You are likely less risk averse and have other typical personality characteristics that have placed you in your current position. You need to consider that employees usually desire the additional level of security and benefits provided by a job. So do not make the assumption that you automatically know what they want. Ask them. Visit with your employees individually about what sort of rewards they would like if the company, or if they achieve certain goals and objectives. Take note and listen. Most of the time, they will give you great information that you can execute based on their input.

One very effective reward strategy is peer recognition. Employees want to know that you have noticed their extra efforts. Pat them on the back and thank them personally. In addition, recognise their performance in front of their peers. Let everyone know the value they have brought to your business. For most people, this public recognition far exceeds a cash payment in motivational value. With proper incentives in place based on what your employees truly value, you will generate a more responsive workforce that you can count on to deliver what your company promises.

Take Action

The famous marketer Dan Kennedy, has a great saying that I have posted on my office wall.

"Are you still collecting information or are you doing something"

This chapter collects a lot of business shaping information, so... "are you doing something?!" Adopt a few of the techniques I have described and implement them in your work environment. You will see an immediate improvement in all facets of your life and business.

Does your business drain your time and energy and not give you financial rewards for your efforts? Is this what you envisioned when you first opened your doors? If not, then you should review my Business Autopilot system. This system helps you regain some personal time and gets your staff "locked and loaded." Defining what you want for your business ultimately adds asset value and positions you for the future. If and when you want to sell, your business will be worth substantially more than it is now.

7

The Four Primary Ways to Grow Your Business

O NE of the most important things for any business owner, manager, entrepreneur or professional to realise, is that there are four principal ways to grow a business – any business. Of course, there are a myriad of ways you can grow your business. Other than some administrative functions however, some of which are not under your direct influence or control, nearly everything you do to build or grow your business can be classified under four distinct categories. If you learn to apply these simple concepts believe me, your competition won't stand a chance. Why? Because your competitors not only don't understand these concepts, most of them have never even heard of them.

1. Get More Customers

This first method of growing your business is obvious. Get more customers. That's it. Build your customer base by converting more prospects into paying clients. When more people buy from you, you take in more gross dollars, and as a result (depending on your margins and overhead), you make more bottom line profits. As a spin-off benefit, the more people you add to your customer base the more people you have to mine for additional sales. In addition, you also have an increased opportunity for more referrals.

How Most Businesses Attract New Customers

Most business owners including your competition and probably you as well, spend most of their time, effort and money attracting new customers. If you've been in business for any length of time, you probably already know that getting new customers is not always the easiest, most efficient, or most profitable activity you can do.

Each business, industry, or profession has their own methods and timing to contact those who are most likely to be interested in their products and services. For example:

Telephone Soliciting - You probably have received your fair share of calls from these telemarketers. They tend to call at the most inconvenient times such as just when you are sitting down for dinner. This is a cold calling scheme made from a list. Companies can buy lists, or use their own customer list.

Television Advertising - Chiropractors, car dealers, truck driving schools, and lawyers often take a different approach. Many of them advertise heavily on television, especially during the afternoon hours to attract new customers. They've found that a large part of their intended audience... the people who are most inclined to use their services, watch television during those hours, and it's a cost-effective way to reach them.

What works for some businesses, may or may not work for other businesses in the same or different industries or professions.

Doing What Everyone Else is Doing - Most likely, the method you use is the same method that nearly every other business uses. It's called the, "That's how things are done in our industry or profession," method. Typically, when a person first chooses to go into business they look around and see what everyone else is doing. They imitate their competition in most every detail. They layout their office, shop or place of business just like every other similar type of business they've seen. They also look at what everyone else is doing to market or promote their businesses, products and services, and adopt those same marketing plans and methods as their own. This activity isn't isolated to just a few businesses – nearly every business in most every industry or profession is guilty.

So, who set up that system in the first place? And who says it's right, or that it's the best system for you to use? The fact is that there are an unlimited number of methods of attracting new customers to your business, and your imagination is the only limiting factor.

Some of the best, most productive and cost-effective methods you can use, can be adapted from what others are doing in totally unrelated businesses. Now, this brings up a couple of questions.

First, how observant are you? What are others doing who are in the same business? How effective are they?

Next, look around at what other businesses... unrelated businesses in other fields, industries or professions are

doing. How have they solved their problems? Have you
seen what's working for them? Are there any businesses
that stand out, by doing something different or unusual?
Does everyone utilize the same marketing methods?

Next question: How creative are you? Can you look at
what some of the other businesses are doing, and adapt
(with a few minor changes), their methods to your
business? In other words, if you were brand new, just
starting in business, and had no idea of what anyone
before you had done to attract new customers, what would
you do? How would you go about getting new customers?
Would you use the same methods you use now, or would
you do something completely different?

Let me give you an example of thinking outside the
ordinary and drawing on your creativity to originate new
marketing techniques.

A dentist I consult with specialises in working with
children and their teeth. He loves children. He recognises
that as they get older, they may need braces, they'll
probably get married, and have a spouse and children
that will all need dental care. To appeal to his pint-sized
clients, he set up his reception room with a special, "kid-
height" counter. At the dentist's office, the children are
treated not as second-class citizens, but as equals. When
the children arrive for their appointments, they can
talk directly to the receptionist, transact business (with
the parent's help and supervision), and have a hand in
scheduling their future appointments. This dentist even
decorated his reception area with artwork and pictures
contributed by some of his young patients. How do you
think those young people feel? Well, you probably guessed
it. They absolutely love it there. And they tell their
friends about it, too.

As for their parents, they're thrilled! Imagine, having your kids want to go to the dentist! And who do you think the parents use for their own dentist? That's right, the same one their children use. A method this dentist uses to reach more clients is to expand his services to include the parents of his patients. By including adults in his practice, as the kids grow up and have families of their own he has a built-in market. Which dentist do you think they'll use? Their childhood dentist with whom they feel comfortable. They'll insist their spouse switches over, and they'll bring their own children, too.

The relationship this dentist is building with those young people... of friendship, of trust and of caring, will provide him all the financial security he'll ever need. He will be able to do whatever he wants, and go wherever he pleases for the rest of his life.

So, what about you and your business? What are you doing? Specifically, what marketing methods are you using right now to attract new customers and to build lasting relationships with them so they'll do business with you for a lifetime? You also need to consider how many different marketing methods do you presently, and concurrently, have working for you? There's a real danger in having just one or two main methods of attracting new customers.

For example, one of my consulting clients depended almost entirely on a telemarketing team to acquire leads for their salespeople to follow up. When a well-funded competitor opened for business not far away, they hired away nearly all that business' telemarketing staff. and nearly shut the business down. This action nearly shut the business down. When they called me in as a consultant, I could see that we had to do something quickly, just to save the business. We got to work, hired and trained a whole new telemarketing crew, and got the business up and running again. But then we looked at other marketing options and put together an effective direct-mail program, started a proactive referral-generating system, and worked out some joint ventures and host-beneficiary relationships with other, complementary, but non-competing businesses. Now, if something happens to any one of their marketing methods, they have other strategies or other "pillars" in place that can keep the business from collapsing, and keep it running smoothly.

To be sure that you will not experience a similar disaster in your business, consider expanding your marketing methods. To evaluate how you can increase the number of ways you reach customers, start by going back and revisiting the questions I asked earlier. See if there are some areas where you can improve. Make sure you're not dependent on only one or two main methods of attracting new customers.

Attracting new customers to your business is absolutely vital... not only to the growth of your business, but to its very survival. It's critical that you have multiple systems in place so if anything unexpected happens, your business continues running, and growing, uninterrupted. Because of the limited amount of space in these pages, we can't talk about all the methods of getting new customers, but in the training materials and workshops we conduct, we go into great detail on effective ways to attract prospects by the bushel, and convert them into loyal, long-term customers.

The importance of getting new customers cannot be discounted however, there are still three more methods you can use to grow your business. Each of these methods are more profitable, more effective, and give you greater potential for leverage than the first method.

2. Get Your Customers to Make Larger Average Purchases

One of the best ways to grow your business is to increase the amount of your average transaction. Get your customers to spend more money when they buy something from you. This just happens to be the quickest and easiest way to increase your profits. I am continually amazed at the number of businesses that have extensive and expensive plans in place to acquire more customers. Yet, very few have paid much attention to this highly profitable, and highly leveragable step. Simply increase the size of the order, and get more money from each of your customers every time they buy from you.

Up-Selling and Cross-Selling

If you think for a minute about how easy this is and how profitable it can be, you'll see why it's such a powerful concept. One industry which has embraced and mastered this powerful technique is the fast food industry. Nearly every fast-food restaurant incorporates up-selling and "cross-selling" principles in their order system. Think about your own fast-food restaurant experience. You drive up to the speaker and place your order... a sandwich and a drink. Next, a voice comes back over the speaker and asks if you'd like an apple pie, or fries with your order.

That's a classic example of cross-selling, or selling an

additional product in addition to, or beyond the initial purchase. They might also suggest that you "super-size" or "giant-size" your order. This is an example of an up-sell... increasing the size of the initial order. In any case, if you take them up on their suggestion, what they've done is just increase their profits substantially.   They made an additional sale, with no acquisition or marketing costs.

This industry realises that a certain percentage of their customers will say, "yes." And the only reason they say, "yes," is because a suggestion was made to them. So they play the numbers game. By being aware of what their customers might want, but may not ask for on their own, and then by asking questions or making suggestions, they bring in a substantial number of dollars. Other than the actual cost of the product, those dollars are pure profit.

Bundling

Another technique fast food restaurants frequently use is called "bundling," or "packaging."
They combine a sandwich, a drink and fries, and throw in a couple of "bonus" items, like maybe a cookie and a toy. They put it all together in one package, and give it a name like "Happy Meal" in the case of McDonald's. They'll charge you less for that package than what each of those items purchased separately would have cost, but the total dollar amount you spend will be higher. Since there were no marketing costs involved, just product cost, it's pure profit and goes straight to their bottom line.

Applying to your Business

Now, how can you apply this principle to your business? You may not be in the fast food business, but the same principles still apply. Just ask yourself this question: "What additional products or services do you have that would be natural complements to what your customers initially buy from you?" You probably already know possible answers to that question for your own business. For instance, if you have the type of business that offers more than one product to your customers you have a tremendous advantage to capitalise on the up-selling, cross-selling and bundling techniques. Some types of businesses, such as insurance companies that may offer only one type of product or service can also benefit from these strategies. They can package certain policies that cover multiple family members, add riders, or include other complementary services that go beyond the actual policies themselves. Once explained, these concepts seem obvious, but it's surprising how few businesses make effective use these three simple techniques.

Developing Customer Loyalty

As a reputable business, you have an obligation to your customers. These people, who hand over their hard earned money to you, trust you to provide them good quality products and services. They rely on you to give them sound advice and make sure they get the very best value, use and enjoyment from their original purchase. If you have additional products or services that can enhance their purchase, then you should do everything reasonable and ethical to see that they at least have the option of taking advantage of those items. Again, it's playing the numbers game. Only a percentage of your customers will take advantage of your offer. But at least you will have given them the opportunity, and you will have fulfilled your obligation to them.

When applying this concept to your business, be sure

you train your employees properly. You need to be sure you don't make the decision for your customers. Give them a choice, and let them decide. If you come across as sincere, and not pushy, they'll realise that you are really trying to do them a favour. They will see you as helping them get more value, more use, and more benefit from their decision and their purchase. With this no pressure sincere approach, your customers will come back to do business with you again, and again, and will refer others to you, as well.

Up-selling, cross-selling and bundling are only three of more than a dozen immediate, profit-producing methods you can use to skyrocket your business to the next level. If you do nothing more than find a way to incorporate these three techniques in your business (which you should be able to do within the next twenty-four hours), you'll blast your profits completely through the roof.

Think about it... increasing your sales... increasing your profits... without increasing your expenses. It's an exciting concept, and it can add an immediate twenty, thirty, even forty percent or more, in pure profits to your bottom line!

3. Get Your Customers to Buy From You More Often

In other words, increase the frequency of their purchases. Get them to come back, Give them reasons to want to come back and to continue doing business with you. The longer your customers go between purchases from you, the more chance they have of buying from your competition.

The adage, "Out of sight, out of mind," applies in this case. You need to keep your name constantly in front of your customers. Use educational information, notices of changes in the law, or updates regarding the products or services they've purchased from you that can affect them. Tell them about new products, new lines, special incentives and other offers that might benefit them.

This idea works two-fold.

> It "locks" your customers in, so they can't afford to do business with anyone else.
>
> It makes it so attractive to do business with you, that they wouldn't even consider going anywhere else.

What you really want to do, is lead your customers to the inescapable and undeniable conclusion, that they would have to be completely out of their minds to even consider doing business with anyone else but you. This transcends your selection of products or services, the prices you charge, your location, or any relationship they may have with another business.

Let me give you some real life examples of how this works: One of the clients I consult with owns a restaurant. For his business customers who like to take their clients to lunch, he offers a certain number of lunches for a pre-paid, discounted price. By doing this, he "locks in" his customer, gets his money up-front, and makes it convenient for everyone. The customer simply signs the check, which includes the tip. No money changes hands during or after the lunch, and new customers are constantly being introduced to his restaurant. As a result, many of those new customers take advantage of the same arrangement for their clients.

Here's another example. The car wash where I take my cars offers a special pre-paid, discounted card, that's good for a certain number of car washes. It's a great deal for me. I save money and I can take my car to be washed when it's convenient, even if my teenagers have gotten into my wallet and taken my last couple of dollars. When my card is filled, I've got a free wax job coming. It's a good deal for the car wash company as well. They've gotten their money up front and have locked me in as a loyal customer and away from the competition.

Here's one more. The store where my wife buys shoes offers a "points" program. Every so often, she receives a notice in the mail informing her of how many points she's accumulated. Even if she has not been to that store for quite a while, when she gets the notice and sees the credit she has coming, she nearly always makes it back to that store within a couple of days. In addition, she hardly ever leaves empty handed.

Airlines offer upgrades and mileage bonuses for those who fly with them on a regular basis. Countless other businesses offer similar programs as well. So how do you apply this concept to your business? Think about what would:

> Endear your customers to you
> Lock them in
> Get them coming back more often
> Encourage referrals

For example:

Do you have an educational newsletter or special informative reports that you periodically send that keeps your customers updated on the latest news in your industry?

Do you send postcards, or do you have a website that keeps them informed of new items and promotions?

Do you hold special "Customer Appreciation Sales" or events?

Do you have a frequent buyer club for your more loyal customers?

Do you offer a Referral Reward system that recognises or compensates your customers for referring their friends?

All these features let your customers know that you value and appreciate them and that you want them to come back. Make doing business with you fun, risk-free, rewarding, and easy!

By these suggestions, I'm sure you can see that the ideas are unlimited. While the restaurant, car wash and shoe store examples may not apply directly to your business, they should spark some ideas. You know your business and market better than anyone. Use these examples to generate your own program to develop trust and loyalty from your customers.

In our coaching programs we go into great detail, and discuss more than two-dozen very specific strategies that create an almost magnetic effect, that keeps your customers returning time and time again. We lead you by the hand and help you develop personalised and effective strategies that keep them saying, "I'll be back"... strategies that keep them "insulated" from, and locked out of your competition.

4. *Extend Your Customers' "Average Buying Lifetime"*

This concept, known as "Customer Retention" refers to a measure of the average amount of time you keep a customer? How long do they continue doing business with you before they move on? Are they one-time buyers? Do they stay with you for a year, five years or ten years? Have you ever even stopped to figure this out? This is an important step, and one that we'll be discussing in more detail in later pages.

Next, what are you doing in your business right now, to make sure your customers continue doing business with you? If you don't have a strategic plan, a working system in place, you are going to lose a certain percent of your current customers to the competition. There's no doubt about it. Your competition... right now... right this very minute, is making plans and taking steps to take your customers away from you. The question you need to ask yourself is not, "What are you going to do about it?" The real questions are:

"What are you currently doing about it?"
"What are you doing about it right now?"

Essentially, what plans... what systems do you have in place to keep your customers from defecting to the competition? Let's talk about your customers for a minute. Are they thrilled enough with the products you offer and the services they receive from you to continue doing business with you year after year? If you answer "yes" to that question, my next questions would be:

"Are you sure?"
"How do you know?"

"Where did you get your information?"
"How reliable is it?"
"Can you explain in detail, the system you have in place for finding out?"

Notice that I said, "Are they thrilled enough?" Not "are they satisfied enough?" There's a big difference between being thrilled and being satisfied in your customers and it affects you right on the bottom line. Last year, more than 200 million Americans stopped doing business with companies with whom they were "satisfied." Sixty percent of so-called "satisfied" customers switch companies or brands on a regular basis.

As a business owner, you can't afford not to thrill your customers and to build their trust in you and your business while you're at it. The cost is too high, and unfortunately, most business owners simply don't understand this point. Let's take a look at what the potential cost could be to you if you fail to do these things. Let's say that you make $200 in sales per year from your average customer. Let's also assume that for any number of reasons, 100 customers stop doing business with you each year. They may die or move away. They may no longer have need for your products or services. They may switch companies, have a relative in the business, or possibly have a bad experience with someone in your company.

They may just simply disagree with some policy or procedure you might have. It could be a falling out with a staff member or employee, a personality conflict, a miscommunication, a problem they had with one of your products, or perhaps a feeling of neglect from you or someone in your business. It really doesn't matter what the reason, they just stop doing business with you. This means those 100 customers are no longer paying you $200 this year which just cost you $20,000.

Now let's factor in word of mouth referral. What if those 100 customers tell 5 others about their experience with you? That's an additional 500 potential customers who won't be doing business with you this year (or maybe ever again, for that matter). What if each of them had been spending an average of $200 per year with your company? That's $100,000 you won't be receiving from them, PLUS the $20,000 you lost on your existing customers who left. That brings the total in lost income to $120,000 in just one year!

It's not unusual for some businesses to bring in a hundred (or more) new customers each month. That's twelve hundred-plus new customers a year. Out of the new customers they attracted to their business, they may only see a total increase in their customer base of 150 or 200 at year-end (sometimes not even that).

What happened to the other 1,000 plus customers? Where did they go? Surely, they all didn't die, or move away. Interestingly, most business owners don't concern themselves with what, or whom they've lost. They just focus on their net gain. They figure that if they finish the year with more customers or more sales than they started with, they're ahead.

Now, let's return to the original 100 lost customers. Suppose you give them reasons… good, compelling, life or business enhancing reasons, to continue doing business with you this year. Let's also suppose that each of them told those same five people about their now-positive experience with you. You now have the $20,000 you would have lost in the first place, and another $100,000 you may possibly pick up from their referrals or by word of mouth testimonials. For most businesses, this extra income could be put to good use.

The point is, customers are important – all customers. In fact, they're critical. A business couldn't remain in business unless it has someone to buy its products and services. Those "someone's" are real people like you and me. If you sell your products to the business community, remember, businesses don't buy from businesses. People in business buy from other people in business. Your market is always people, not businesses.

In summary, we've covered a lot of ground and a lot of ideas. So, let's pause for a minute, and recap what we've discussed up to this point. There are four primary ways to grow a business.

> First, get more customers. And as I mentioned, this is a vital step. But it's also the most difficult and the most costly.

> Second, get your customers to spend more money with you... increase the average transactional value of each sale. And remember that this is the fastest and the easiest way to add immediate profits to your bottom line.

> Third, get your customers coming back to buy from you more often.

> Fourth, extend your customers' buying lifetime. Find ways to retain them, keep them as customers and keep them coming back as long as you possibly can.

It's really pretty simple. Nearly everything you do to build and grow your business can be slotted under one of these four categories. As I mentioned earlier, there are more than two-dozen ways to apply these concepts and build your business, but for now, if you'll work on these four primary methods, you'll absolutely run circles around your competitors.

As you take a good, close-up look at these four areas, you'll see that what it really boils down to is effectively marketing your business to your customers and potential customers.

In the end, the success of your business enterprise depends, largely, on how effectively you market your business.

> If you want your business to excel...
> If you want to virtually eliminate your competition...
> If you want to become the dominating force in your marketplace...

Then you've got to begin thinking of yourself as being in the marketing business, not in the product or service selling business.

As I've advised you before, you need to consider yourself as the head of a marketing organisation that sells the products and services that your business offers. Once you begin operating effectively at that point, you'll find that your job becomes much easier and much more enjoyable. Your prospects and customers will begin seeking you out and referring others to you, rather than you chasing after them. The net result will be that your marketing costs will plummet, and your profits will skyrocket!

Take Action Exercise

Most business owners know exactly how much they have invested in furniture, fixtures and equipment. They can tell you, nearly to the penny, how much each item costs, how old it is, how much it has depreciated and its remaining life expectancy. That's important information for any business to have. What's amazing is that very few business owners know the value of their most important asset... their customers. Think about how this whole concept relates to your business. How can you specifically extend your customer's buying lifetime with you?

Take a few minutes and answer these questions?

> First of all, who are your customers ... those who are buying from you now?
> Who are their family members?
> Do you know the names and ages of their spouse or children?
> Do you know where they work?
> Do you know where their spouse works?
> Do you know where their children attend school?
> What are their hobbies or interests?
> Do you know why they purchased a certain type of product or service?
> Do you know who their friends, neighbors or relatives are?
> On the service end of your business, do you know how your employees treat or feel about your customers?
> Do they, or do you, for that matter, have favorite customers?
> What makes them a "favorite?"
> Is it how much they spend?
> How often they come in?

Their personality?

How do you treat those customers?

Do you treat them any differently than the others?

Do you have regular staff meetings and talk about how to think like a customer?

What you would want if you were a prospect considering doing business with you for the first time?

Do existing customers consider giving repeat business to your establishment or organization?

Would they consider referring a friend, a family member or an acquaintance?

Do you have a training system in place to teach your staff how to handle or deal with difficult customers? (I.e. short-tempered customers or analytical customers.)

Do you have a plan for moving people up the "Loyalty Ladder?" From Suspect to Prospect to Shopper.

Then on to Customer, Client, and Advocate, finally converting them into Raving Fans?

When a customer stops doing business with you, do you know why?

Do you have a system in place to find out?

What would you have to do differently to get your customers to buy from you for, say, 5 ½ years, instead of just 5 years?

Take a few minutes and go through these questions and formulate answers for them. Incorporate that information into your business practices. You can work wonders towards extending the buying lifetime of your customers. And as a result, you'll add significant profits to your bottom line.

8

Modeling for Success

THE concept of business modeling has been around since the 1950's, but has only received popular usage in the 1990's. Modeling is basing the different aspects of your business off the concepts used by other businesses. This includes its products and services, strategies, infrastructure, organisation and operational procedures and policies. There are really just four key business modelling areas that are successful.

Cloning
Leverage
Using a Mentor
Prototyping and Testing

Cloning

Why would you want to invent something? Why would you want to be a pioneer? Both are fraught with risk because you are going where no one has gone before. If you want a successful business, it is much more logical to duplicate what works for somebody else, and then be innovative. You can apply your own ideas to a proven concept that can be grown quickly with massive value. There is nothing wrong with borrowing ideas even from outside your industry if they work, and then making them better.

117

Cloning is simply taking what works somewhere else and copying it almost exactly. The danger is that you become a "me too." For example, if you are in the business of providing product X, and you look at every other product X company and say, "Well, if that is what they do then I need only do the same thing." That is not going work. It may get you started and attract some business, but it is not likely to launch your business into an exponential rate of growth. So, be careful about what you do with an idea. If you use an idea from another company, do not copy it exactly, put your own unique stamp on it and make it different. Make it better.

Creative Swiping

A similar idea is what they call "creative swiping". We all do it in one way or another. Say that you read an article or a book or see something on TV that contains a good idea for your business. Then grab it as your own. I mean, there is a difference between creative swiping and plagiarism. Plagiarism is where you promote the idea or words that you swiped as your own; whereas, creative swiping is taking the idea and saying, "Hey, I learned this great idea the other day from Rich Schefren, but here is what I am going to do with it." Give credit where it is due. I'm a great fan of creative swiping because I do not think it is wise to be completely original. I think it is much better to start with a proven idea and build upon it as opposed to being completely original. The risk ratio is far less.

Copywriting

Another area from which you can garner ideas is copywriting. They do not call it copywriting for nothing. Headlines of other ads can be particularly useful. As

I said before, headlines are very important to your marketing because they are the first thing people read in your advertisements, perhaps the only thing. Well, if you think it is apropos to what you want to say, there is nothing wrong with stealing the idea behind somebody else's headline. For instance: the idea behind the "Who Wants to be a Millionaire?" title for the TV show could well translate to a fashion store advertisement saying: "Who Wants to be a Fashion Queen?"

Leverage

Leverage is another great tool for modelling. It means getting more with less. You can leverage many things: typically people; processes; technology; time; and capital.

Leveraging People

So, how do you leverage people? As I have pointed out previously, if you estimate that your time is worth $400 or more per hour, and you can get your work done by somebody that is paid $20 per hour, you are leveraging people. Another example is if you have a worker who is paid $60 per hour in your business, and you systemise what they do so that a $40 per hour person can do that job. You can then organize it so that the $60 per hour person can do the job of a $90 per hour. This is leveraging people.

Leveraging Processes

Can you leverage a process? Absolutely! Create systems to streamline tasks and use technology to automate various processes. If done properly this reduces the skilled workers needed, and greatly increases productivity per worker. The use of technology in general and automation in particular in business is a book in itself.

Leveraging Time

Time once lost can never be regained. It is your most precious resource and one of the easiest to squander needlessly. Leveraging time is all about getting maximum value from this perishable commodity. Business owners often do not allocate their time wisely. They spend time on a variety of activities many of which are needless or could be delegated. If you are spending time on unimportant tasks, you are not earning up to your potential. When you understand how to leverage, you will begin to earn more money for your time.

Leveraging your time is also about moving you and your company toward your goals. If you are spending your time effectively, you will be applying your time to meaningful activities that get you closer to your destination. If you are not, you have room for improvement.

Leveraging Capital

Again, this is using money to make more money. Using money you don't have or borrowing money is one way to go. You can use these funds to buy capital goods or real estate for your business. These assets hopefully appreciate enough or increase your business turnover enough so that the gain pays off the loan interest and perhaps also creates a cash profit. You can also use such loan money to buy out competitors or other businesses. The basic idea is to use loan money as leverage to increase the value of your business. This can be a great money making strategy in a stable or rising market.

Using a Mentor

The third skill for modeling success is to use a mentor. A metaphor to illustrate this concept is "learning to fly under the wings of eagles." How do you find the right mentor? How do you find somebody who is willing to help you out? Since I first entered the business work force, I have always tried to have a mentor. It is surprisingly easy. In so many cases, you merely have to ask. If you come across someone at a seminar or are acquainted with them slightly as a fellow business person, simply make your approach and say directly: "Well, I really enjoyed what you said at the seminar" or "I really admire the way you run your business. Is it possible that I could buy you lunch or buy you a coffee and just ask you a few questions?" There are not too many people who would actually say no to that. Most people who are good at something are only too happy to see their prowess appreciated. For the most part, they also like to pass those skills on to anyone interested enough to ask. Even people who are in exactly the same industry or are operating a similar business, even in a close suburb, will be pleased to help if asked. So ring, write, whatever you need to do, but asking is the first step. If you don't ask, nothing will happen. It is the first rule of negotiation. Ask for what you want.

Now, what if you can not get a mentor? No problem. There are many people that you can use for coaching support. I find no difficulty in paying for good mentoring and coaching support. The way I see it I am leveraging my time. I leverage my time by spending some money now and getting the advice straight away. I do not have waste time figuring it out. That to me is a good exchange; I am exchanging my money for time.

Prototyping and Testing

Lastly on modeling for success is prototyping and testing. The idea is to always try to test new ideas or systems or products as quickly and cheaply as possible. An example that I recently had to deal with was a new website. They can be very expensive to build, and if you get it wrong, even more expensive to fix. So what I did was just to get the graphics done roughly on paper along with how the copy and buttons would work, and then show it to a number of customers to see if they thought it got the right message across and would be easy to navigate. Using this prototype allowed me to deal with many mistakes before they were fatally incorporated into the real thing.

Google Adwords

Another excellent method of testing web ideas is Google Adwords. In Google Adwords, you can test two ideas at the same time through split testing. You can put up an ad on a keyword and, if somebody clicks it, you know that the customer is interested in what your ads says. If you use two different ads and you split test if one gets twice as many clicks as the other, you are then on your way to creating the best ad to get the customers clicking. The next thing is, if they click on your ad, they go to a website. If that website asks them a question and offers to give them something if they answer that question, it is like doing a survey. So, what is the point? Not only are you testing different headlines in your Google Adwords, but you are also getting a survey that tells you what customers are likely to want. You now not only have a list of what people want, but also an idea of what headline might attract them in the first place. That is very powerful and it is very cheap.

Appealing to Women

Another, even more cost effective survey is to pitch any new ideas for the business to your partner. If you haven't got a partner, ask a female acquaintance, and pay attention to what she says. From my experience, you are likely to get a really accurate answer, but you may not like it. If so, don't get upset, she is probably right. Studies show that in almost all buying decisions it is women who have the last word. I don't care what type of business you have, somewhere down the line it is most likely a woman who will make the final buying decision.

I can almost hear you say, "Well, that is not true. I buy the car and I buy the house." Be truthful. Did you make the decision without their influential input? Not likely. In any case, it's right in the broad view, and it pays businessmen to take that fact into consideration. Design everything you do in your business to be attractive to women.

Now, you are thinking: what about a car mechanic or any other male-oriented industry? Perhaps, but what harm is there in making your premises attractive to women. Car mechanics certainly have to deal with as many women as men dropping off their cars for repair. In addition, any such service facility worth its salt will have a clean and tidy waiting room with as many women's magazines in the rack as there are men's. The point of all this is to convince you that you can't go wrong designing your business with a female perspective in mind regardless of what business you're in. Of course, that doesn't mean that everything is in shades of pink. It just means clean and attractive enough to make a woman feel relaxed.

As an example of businesses adopting a female perspective, one of the areas that I have been heavily involved in is in customer service call centers. They have large staffs with a high percentage of women. It sounds strange now, but back in 1997 or '98, I was laughed at when I suggested that all the bathrooms should be cleaned at least twice a day. I insisted that especially the women's restrooms be spotless with hand creams and even fresh flowers. It certainly kept the women happy, and that goes a long way to keeping everybody happy. It also helped keep staff turnover at an industry low.

Take Action Exercises

1. Gather a sampling of all your marketing materials and give them to three females that you don't know and that are not associated with your business. Ask them if they could make comments as to the way the documents look, do they make sense, are they easy to understand, etc. Be prepared to make changes when you read their responses, especially if they all agree.

2. What are three successful businesses that you admire? Why? What do they do that you do not? How could you incorporate just one of there methods into what you do?

9
Systemisation

SYSTEMISING your business is the ultimate key to shaping up your business and preparing it for sale. The process of systemising your business can be a closely held secret and carefully guarded. So, the following pages contain information that is critical to helping you design your business for maximum profit. I want to start by introducing you to a simple approach for systemisation. This is an easy one that you can implement quickly with "non-critical" aspects of your business. I'll show you how to get some benefits now, so you then will be more comfortable with the system approach and thus be able to focus on the important areas of your business. As soon as you see the ease with which it can be applied, you'll be comfortable to go on to bigger & more important areas of your business.

Jump Start

The Jump Start process will help you eliminate repetitive, pressing problems – particularly ones that push your emotional buttons – by focusing on system failures, not personal failures.

The Jump Start process gets rid of the "blame game," a natural human reaction when things go wrong. We all look to blame someone or something when difficulties arise, when the real answer is that there is a system missing.

The Jump Start helps you fix that problem or frustration quickly. And I guarantee that it's not just a temporary fix. When you use systems thinking, you will be able to identify and permanently eliminate the underlying causes of your problem.

The Jump Start serves three objectives:

> It teaches you to think systematically.
> It helps you eliminate work-related frustrations in a way that prevents their recurrence.
> It frees up valuable time and energy, you can better use to focus attention on other important matters.

This common-sense approach has two underlying ideas:

> First, everything we do in the business can be systemised, and
> Second, people are never the problem, only the lack of systems.

For instance, a business owner who thinks that a lack of clients is due to market conditions or a poor economy is missing the point. I would say that the more likely cause is the lack of a lead-generation system.

Too many people take the "fire-fighter" approach to problem solving. First they wait until the fire has truly got a hold, and then they think that dousing the fire is all that needs to be done. Putting the fire out will surely relieve the problem, but often the cause of the fire is still threatening because non-systematic solutions rarely scale well. For example, when your sales volume increases, the problems almost always get worse. At this point, the fire re-ignites, leaving the business in worse shape than before.

Systematic approaches, using processes, tools and data that ANYONE (with a reasonable level of skill) can operate, tend to scale much better.

The ability to scale or handle more volume is one of the biggest benefits of systemisation.

Naturally, we both know that not all problems and frustrations are systems-related. There will be legitimate personality conflicts, emotional issues, and differences in operating styles that have nothing to do with systems. The Jump Start however, provides consistent ways to recognise which are systems issues and which are people issues.

If the next time you encounter a problem in your business, your immediate reaction is to ask what system is missing, rather than to blame somebody, you'll know you're on the right track.

I know, of course, that people sometimes are the problem. And, if you are using a systems solution, it will be clear to you too just who is unwilling or unable to operate your system. This is because it will highlight the "people problem" in a way that is objective, dispassionate and without blame, allowing you to take appropriate measures.

In the Jump Start, the terms "system" and "process" are NOT the same. The difference is that, although a system is a process, it is a process that relies on tools and data, not just individual expertise and experience.

A system can also be documented. Only systems can be written down so that they can be retrieved and duplicated whenever necessary. Thus a good system can produce consistent, predictable results each time it is executed. High levels of skill are also not needed to operate a system so that it produces comparable results time after time.

The Jump Start is a system – a system for designing systems. It is 7-Step process of evaluating the frustration, identifying the underlying problem, and creating a system-based solution.

Let me say, your first few applications of the Jump Start may seem awkward, as do most new things. But you will quickly adapt to it, and soon the whole process will seem natural.

The seven Jump Start steps are:

1. What's on your mind? What is frustrating you?
2. Restate the problem as a system problem
3. Uncover and quantify the underlying business condition
4. Identify the general system solution
5. Affirm your commitment to solve the problem
6. Define the specific system solution
7. Implement the solution

I want to first point out that this process is designed to come up with general solutions before specific solutions. This is deliberate. If you focus too quickly on specific solutions, it will hamper your efforts to prioritise problems. You may even find that your time and energy are spent on situations that aren't pressing or even worth resolving.

TIP: Beware of jumping to conclusions. When first looking at a solution to your frustrations, it's easy to jump to answers. Follow the Jump-Start process fully and the answers are likely to be more relevant and easier to implement.

Step 1 – What's on your Mind? What is Frustrating you?

Let's get started. Begin by identifying your sources of frustration. To get you thinking along the right lines, here are some other examples of frustrations and their (possible) general solutions:

Frustration: "I'm the only one that can do this"

General Solution: A process to educate and train others on what I do

Frustration: "I don't know what my conversion rates are"

General Solution: A system to measure my marketing campaigns and provide reports.

Make a Small List
Identify what's on your mind and what's frustrating you. The ordinary business owner has many issues or frustrations bouncing around in his head right now. For instance:

I wish my staff would clean-up at the end of the day.
What problems will Bill cause tomorrow?
I never know how my marketing is going.
These will give you an idea of typical frustrations that you may be experiencing. Think about your business and your

daily concerns and make a small list of these frustrations. Don't be too wordy, just make a simple list. Remember, you don't have to write down major problems, just start with small annoyances.

This step is important. You need to state your frustrations in very specific language. Avoid broad general terms, or blaming someone or something. The reason for this is if you state your frustration in the wrong way, it can lead you down an incorrect path, possibly to a solution that doesn't result in a cure for the frustration.

TIP: If you ask someone what their problems are - they will generally tell you one of two things. 1) What they think you want to hear and 2) What they think is the solution to the issue. The challenge is to determine what the underlying issue or problem is and disregard what they actually said. Can you do that with yourself?

Once you can be clear as to what the actual frustration or problem is you have half a chance of being able to apply many solutions.

Select a Frustration to Address
Now pick one of them to work on right now that you'd like to be rid of right away.

Go on to the next step.

Step 2 - Restate the Frustration as a System Problem

This step looks self-explanatory, but sometimes isn't. I've found that when we conduct Autopilot Advisory Services with clients, this step can sometimes take some explanation.

To put it simply, your frustration is almost never a person, vendor or your problem; it is a system problem.

If you describe your frustration as "I can't" or "we don't", then you're thinking about the frustration in terms of you or someone else. You're blaming.

You must get yourself out of the equation if you are to convert a frustration to a system problem. You must shift your focus to what is not working, and not your part in it.

For example, say your original frustration is: "Many clients waste my time and don't buy." The question is: Who keeps wasting time? If you answer is: clients, you are wrong. The problem is that you need a way to qualify who is a potential client and who is not before spending too much time with them. If you look at the problem from a system perspective, the answer is: "I need a system to qualify prospects."

Now you have a clear, concise, system-directed statement of the problem, which brings you into the heart of the Jump Start.

Step 3 - Uncover and Quantify the Frustrating Issue

How do you uncover the specific issue that's causing your frustration? You must ask many specific questions that will quantify the underlying conditions; questions such as how much, how many, for how long, what percentage. In other words: get the facts.

There's no doubt you will be surprised by the answers, because quantification often reveals very different conditions than those you thought existed. Understanding the hard details will help you to develop priorities objectively.

Now, to get started, ask yourself a good lead off question such as:

> "How does this frustration specifically impact my business?"

You'll find it easier to be specific if you run through a real-life example of the frustration. Another question to ask:

> "What results am I not getting?"

Just think about it a little and you will soon develop your own way of using questions to "feel" your way to the underlying causes of frustrations.

This kind of interrogation will soon uncover not only the real underlying causes of your business frustration, but it will also point you toward a solution or solutions that will truly eliminate that frustration.

Here are some good questions to ask yourself to see if

THE GREAT BUSINESS SHAPE UP

you're close to uncovering the real issue.

> "Why does this bother me?"
> "How do I know that this is an issue?"
> "What evidence is there about this issue?"
> "What am I not getting?"

Until you are clear about what is really happening in your business, there's nothing that can be done. And never fear, as you continue to try to live with the problem, your emotional response to it will escalate and your frustration deepen.

However, by recognising the frustration as a system problem, by insisting on the specific, you will take the first giant steps toward eliminating the emotional charge and actually solving the problem.

Step 4 - Identify the General System Solution

Once you have attained a clear and specific understanding of the frustration you want to fix, the solution will begin to emerge. Then to solidify how this solution should work, the most important element is to be clear about the result you want: you must know exactly what must happen to eliminate the frustration.

Complete the following sentence:

The general solution might be to install a system that will...

For example, if you're frustrated about the difficulty of always having to find new customers, you might write:

"The general solution might be to install a system that sells new products to my existing customers."

If you always get lots of client support requests,

"The general solution might be to install a system that will manage client support requests."

It is not the actual working system that we are looking for here; that comes later. What we are trying to do first is to simply identify the general solution.

Don't underestimate the significance of reaching this point of the process. You should by now have dispensed with notions about people dependency, and transcended the trap of finding fault. You are no longer cowed by outside forces that you can't control. You are able to slice through superficial symptoms to identify and quantify actual, underlying causes and effects. But, most importantly, you have learned to think in a new way.

Step 5 - Affirm your Commitment to Solve the Problem

I would like to point out, that there is more to solving a business problem than just understanding it. To solve it takes generally takes time and energy. You must ask yourself whether you are up to it. Ask yourself:

> "Do I really want to fix this frustrating issue, or would I rather live with it?"
> "Is this one important enough to address right away or will it have to wait?"
> "Will this issue 'fix itself' by addressing another frustration first?"

Certainly there are some times when you have to choose
to solve other problems that will provide greater impact or
relief. But remember, this one will not go away. Some day
in some way it will have to be dealt with.

Step 6 - Define the Specific System Solution

There are eight steps to this development process for
creating new systems. You may not need to follow all
steps for all new systems, but my advice is you won't go
wrong if you stick close to the plan. Sometimes, you will
see that small systems may require very little and larger
systems all the steps and more, but for now it is best to
follow the plan closely.

**1. Design your system to incorporate the following
elements:**

A desired outcome: Decide early what you want
the system to do and what results you're looking for.

A sequence of steps. This is the basis of your
"system". You can often build it from existing ad-hoc
processes or copy from known "best practices". It
is also useful to gather everyone who understands
either the problem or the solution and brainstorm
the possibilities. You might already have a system,
but it isn't being followed. Or it might be being
followed, but badly, and needs to be fixed. Whatever
is the problem; the method must be documented, and
then optimised or repaired. Some systems can be
bought off the shelf and, if necessary, customised to
suit your needs. No matter what you need or decide,
you must ensure that your desired results can be
accomplished using these steps and only these steps.
Try it out with a dry run, and then move into live

tests. When you are satisfied, put the new system into operation and monitor the results – making refinements along the way. For now, keep it simple.

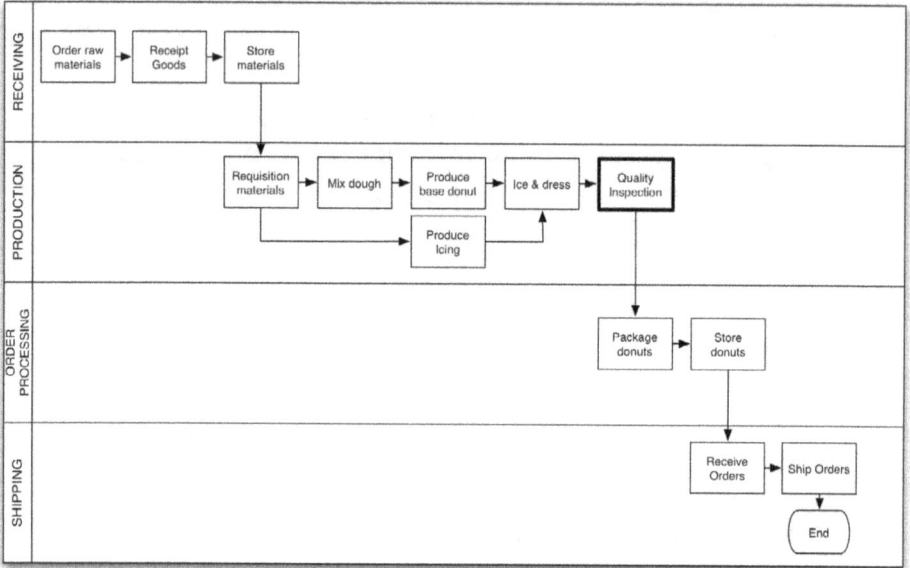

Proper staffing and accountability. If the new system needs input from staff to make it work, don't pick those who already have more to do than they can handle. Assign people to help who have the ability and flexibility to accomplish what needs to be done.

Timing/scheduling/due dates for activities and results. Be realistic but aggressive in implementing your systems. The sooner they are in place, the sooner the benefits will be realised. And don't nitpick. Systems need not be perfect so long as they represent an improvement over what you are doing now.

Standards (requirements, performance criteria, goals). There is little point in setting up a system and then not following it. You must establish your requirements, performance criteria, and goals to measure, track and evaluate its effectiveness once it is installed.

2. Create operating forms and documents such as order forms, documentation of each team member's position, policies, inventory tickets, etc.

3. Write scripts for every key communication. In many cases, a script is the system, which is why scripting is a key element of the Jump Start. The simplest way to develop scripts is to 1) record the process as you describe it to someone else; or 2) record real-life telephone or person-to-person conversations.

4. **Develop tracking and reporting tools** in either printed or digital format. These include quantification, tracking forms, report forms and scheduling calendars, etc. If your people work from home or remote location, web-based forms can be extremely useful.

5. Design a training program that will instruct staff in how to use the system properly. The program can be in written, audio, CD-ROM or even video format (using today's easy-to-use digital video tools). Your first few training sessions can be "live", but this is not a good systems solution, because you may not be present or available when new people join your staff? The best of both worlds is to record your live presentations, and then put them into an easily accessible format.

6. Test your new system. Your training program can be a way of testing your new system. If you have someone, who has never performed this task or activity before, run through each step, using all the diagrams and documents you have developed, you will soon see if it makes sense? Do they get the results required? If not, maybe more work needs to be done on the system.

7. Specify the Implementation Process. Systems that really are systems must be imposed by "executive order". You must take the "Benevolent Dictator" approach. You are the owner, and this new system is not optional; it's mandatory. You must insist that, from now on, this is the new way you do business. That doesn't mean you don't seek staff opinion and incorporate that into your system, but once you're ready to implement, brook no resistance— this is the way it is going to work.

8. Determine the communications and rollout procedure, including positioning of the new system and rollout of its implementation. Use your normal methods for getting the message out - e-mail, intranet or whatever other method you have. There is NO excuse for failing to adhere to system policies, guidelines and rules, so everyone must be adequately informed.

There are some systems you use that will be extremely simple, taking just minutes to create and install from start to finish. For instance, if your frustration involves the inability to identify and take action on important mail, a simple in-box system may be all that's needed. On the other hand, if you consistently run out of parts for your assembly line, you probably have a more complex development project ahead.

Step 7 - Implement the Solution

There is one aspect of this system procedure I would like to stress. Don't waste any time! Implement your new system right away. There will be no benefits until the system is operating.

Be aware, that the system may not produce perfect results at first. You almost always need a certain amount of fine-tuning. You may have missed a step, and you may have to make minor adjustments here and there. The more complex your system, the more likely it will require some work. Systems are dynamic and you will have quantify and track the system's operations and results, and continually seek out ways to improve it.

Executive order or not, the introduction of a new system to those who have to use it should be handled with care. It is normal for people to resist change, and they may find any new system threatening. If they have been involved in the design process of the system, it should be easier. However, not everyone will have been involved. To them, stress the benefits of your new system and appeal to their self-interest. In both the long- and short-term, they will be the people who find that the system makes their jobs easier, more productive and more enjoyable.

Try the following process:

> Introduce the system in a private meeting
> Express your expectations for them
> Get written commitment to honour the system
> Specify the consequences of non-compliance

Celebrate. Your new system is up and running and you have facts to show that it works. Now it's time to celebrate. The process really does work.

Why stop now?

Why not try another Jump Start on one of your other frustrations?

I'll tell you an interesting aspect of systemising your business that often arises at this point in the Jump Start process. If you look back at your original list of frustrations, you may well find that some of the others have already been partly resolved. So many processes are intertwined in any business that resolving one of them will often partly solve the others.

Further Actions

The core business of Portofino Asset Management is working with businesses to get them systemised so the business can run on Autopilot. Our approach is to use our proprietary Business Autopilot System to assist are Advisors & Consultants.

If you'd like some help in getting your business systemised, go to http://systemised.com/

10
Shaping up your Business for Sale

IF you have decided to sell your company as part of your exit strategy, before putting it on the block, you should increase its sales appeal as much as possible. Business brokers call this "dressing up" your firm. This means tidying up any remaining trouble spots with the company that slipped by during your shape up and turnaround. You want to eliminate any possible problems that may influence a potential buyer. Make your company as perfect as possible, turn it into a great takeover candidate which will create the most value for you and your investors.

This chapter details fourteen ways to improve your firm's attractiveness to potential buyers. You may not be able to do them all, but if you miss a few, don't let this deter you from putting your company up for sale if the time is right. You can make many of these fixes concur with the normal sales cycle. Remember selling your business can easily take twelve months, so you should have no trouble adopting most of these suggestions.

Make sure Contracts and Leases are Transferable

Everybody wants an ownership transition to go smoothly. Make sure your contracts and leases are easily transferable to smooth the way to an easy sale. Work with your vendors and landlord to make all agreements automatically transferable to the new owners. It will be a major selling point to prospective buyers.

Remove Excess Inventory and Equipment

During due diligence, obsolete inventory and equipment on the books raises a major warning sign. It usually indicates shoddy controls and a management that overstates its books. Don't wait; write these assets down now, and dispose of the excess inventory and equipment as soon as possible.

Comply with all State and Federal Laws Especially Environmental Rules

Prospective buyers will baulk at purchasing a company that does not comply with current government rules. Putting these problems right is often a time-consuming process. In addition there could be fines and bad press. "Environmental" problems are a prime example. Such problems are notorious for needing expensive cleanups and may engender large lawsuits from the company's neighbours. Deal with them now. You also need to correct any out-of-compliance issues. Do more than correct these issues, ensure that you also have all the official documentation to show that your company is in compliance. You don't want the slightest excuse that will raise a prospective buyer's fears about your company.

Get Costs under Control

Having all areas of your business operating in the most cost effective manner can increase your business' attractiveness to potential buyers. Put a system in place to track your costs and evaluate your suppliers on regular intervals to be sure you are getting the best price for frequently purchased goods and services. Be sure you only cut costs sensibly and not where it will sacrifice quality or production in important areas. The following are the most common areas to evaluate for cost savings:

> Packaging
> Freight / Courier
> Office / Computer Supplies
> Document Storage
> Printing / Stationery
> Telephone / Mobile Phone Costs
> Insurance
> Bank / Interest Charges
> Travel Costs
> Protective Clothing
> Energy Consumption
> Maintenance
> Cleaning / Products
> Waste Disposal
> Hotel / Bar Supplies

Clean, Organise and Paint

Selling a business is much like selling a house: a clean-up and a fresh coat of paint will positively influence prospective buyers. Paint the interior, the outside, and the equipment. Make sure that you have organised everything. Sparkling offices and production areas tell a prospective buyer that you run a top-notch organisation.

As part of this improvement process, make sure your buildings are sound and the equipment works. Don't skimp on your maintenance. Equipment and buildings must be in top condition. The last thing you want is an embarrassing equipment breakdown during due diligence. If your roof leaks, get it fixed. Puddles on the floor can be deal killers. In addition, repair any areas and surfaces that may have been water damaged. Even if a leaking roof is fixed, you should also cover up the evidence so that this is a non issue for a buyer.

Develop a Second-in-Command

Attempting to sell a business that is completely dependent on the owner or CEO can worry prospective buyers. They fear the company will fail to work once you are gone. However, if you have appointed a capable second-in-command this fear will be reduced. As part of this appointment, delegate the daily business tasks to this individual. Don't wait to do this. The longer you have your second-in-command in place, the more valuable your company will become.

Have a Leadership Development Program

Buyers will appreciate that there is a second-in-command, but they will also look for management depth throughout your company. Having to depend on one employee will make them almost as nervous as depending solely upon the business owner. Start a leadership program now so that you will be able to show prospective buyers how you develop top people into senior leadership positions.

Focus on Your Business

Businesses that are too diversified are regarded as a little "iffy" to most prospective buyers. Most want a company that is strong player in a specific industry so that it fills a gap in their portfolio. If you have not focused your business to strongly address a market, you need to do it now. Look to your core business, and focus your energy there.

Have Good Accounting Systems in Place

Quality record keeping and accounting is another important selling point. Producing accurate and reliable information builds general trust in buyers. There is an additional upside in that the buyer does not have to reduce the price because of doubt in the accounting. There is no doubt that superior accounting systems and procedures add value to a firm. If your systems don't meet these criteria, you need to update them as soon as possible. Remember this is not an overnight process and such corrections normally take a few months before the systems works properly.

You should avoid setting up new accounting software right before a putting your business on the market. Installation can be a nightmare, and it could take a year or more before it functions properly. New software needs new procedures and, until it is well bedded in, it will produce poor reports. In general, you can expect at least minor chaos for an appreciable time if you introduce new accounting software.

It is best then not to change your accounting software immediately before marketing your company as a takeover candidate. If you have accounting system problems, try to adapt the current system without making a wholesale software change.

Have an Audit Done by a Reputable CPA Firm

As mentioned above, having trustworthy financial information is the key to getting a good price. Your financial numbers will look absolutely legitimate if you engage a Big Four accounting firm to audit your financial statements and take an independent count of your inventory. Although such an audit can easily cost $30,000 or more, it will give much confidence to any prospective buyer, ensuring them that your company has nothing to hide.

Don't just accept the first price for an audit that you get. Bid it out to get the best deal.

Many of the leading accounting firms also give a large discount to new clients. However, if the price is still too high, consider using a regional firm. They might not have the Big Four's (or Six) credibility, but an audit by a regional firm is much better than no audit at all.

Benchmark against Industry Ratios

Your company financial ratios may not be in line with your industry's averages. This may raise a warning sign to prospective buyers who might worry that something is "wrong" with your company. This will be especially true for ratios related to our working capital and debt. First, know what the financial ratio standards are for your industry. If you have trouble, contact your trade association as they may have this information. Once you have the information, change your business to match these figures as closely as possible.

Develop a Diversified Client Base

Buyers are wary of a company dependent on only one or two customers. The problem that worries them is that once you leave the company, the customer might transfer its business to a competitor. This is not an unreasonable fear, since you probably have developed a strong relationship with your primary client. To forestall such a scenario, you should try to diversify your client base as much as possible.

I would suggest that, ideally, no client should represent more then 10% of your business. Although it may be impossible to do this before you sell the company, it is always worthwhile goal.

Develop Competitive Advantages

Prospective buyers will be reluctant to look at your company unless it is strong and has competitive advantages. By definition, your company must have some or it would not have survived its turnaround. However, they might not be as evident as you would want. You must endeavour to make them noticeable, while also developing new ones that buyers want. Examples of clear competitive advantages are patents, strong brand identity, exclusive products, unique sales channels and prime locations.

Update Your Business & Marketing Plan

The business plan that you have developed can be more than a great guidance tool. It is also a great sales feature for your company. Its study will give potential buyers a deep understanding of your management's estimate of the company's potential and a road map to reach it.

Your business plan is where you can clearly identify your competitive advantages, and describe your strategy for keeping and growing a significant market share.

Take Action Exercises

1. Where are you in each of these areas? Rate yourself on a 0 to 10 scale. What would you business look like if you rated > 5? What about if you were rated > 9?

2. What could you business be valued at if you rated > 9?

11
Work-Life Balance

STRIKING the right balance between work and your personal life can be difficult. Whenever you are building a business, the claim on your time can be enormous. It usually requires self sacrifice and the unwavering support of your family for as long as it takes to make the business profitable. This book has been designed to help you know how to grow your business as quickly as possible and to make the best decisions concerning your money and time. It also covers how to systemise your business and help you create massive value in your business. This enables you to plan an exit strategy that makes sense for you and your business. You will have the choice of being able to sell your business for real money and not just have to walk away and abandon your equity. It also accelerates your path to profitability and helps you avoid the numerous pitfalls along the way.

Concentrating on your business is necessary to build a profitable company. But having your head down and working all the time is not healthy, and it is certainly not good for your home life. You must achieve balance in what you do. The concept of work-life balance assumes that you can work efficiently, get a lot done and have your business grow but at the same time enjoy a great home life. This includes an active social life, and balance in all other areas of your life. You may have decided to pursue having your own business for a variety of reasons, but most people simply want a better lifestyle. They want to be able to give their family the security and future that comes from building equity and value in a business. If all you are doing is slaving away as a glorified employee and just barely getting by, that does not ultimately achieve your goals. It just means that you are spending more time working and less time at home, and in the end you will have put your personal life on hold for nothing. This can be a sobering realisation and can place undue stress on all your personal relationships.

Allocate Time to Thinking and Planning

There are many techniques on how to bring back a balance in your life between work and life. One of the best ones that I have ever encountered is simply to spend a half a day each week away from the office and only concentrate on planning. Plan on spending this time away from the office and use it for executing some of the ideas in this book. The more time you can devote to thinking and planning the more benefits you will reap in terms of sanity and happiness in your family.

Be sure to dedicate your thinking time only to thinking. There is a difference between thinking and working, and you should not mix the two. When you are thinking, do not have interruptions that are work related. Insulate yourself from people ringing you up or sticking their head in your office and asking you to help them solve a problem. Thinking time needs to be thinking time. As a start, allocate a half a day a week to thinking and planning and gradually increase your time away from the office. Over time work toward spending three days a week away from the office, managing, planning, and growing your business. The sooner you can do that, the more value you will be creating in your business and the more options you will have for your exit strategy. You will be getting towards your goal of working on your business, not in your business.

Celebration

Incorporate some celebration into your life. Celebrate wins and successes with your staff your vendor partners and your family. You don't have to invite everyone to the same party or the same function, but you should get into a habit of really building some enjoyment into what you are doing. You will find that when you come home from your business, that you are actually in a happy mood and not grumpy from the constant draining work. You will not be constantly worrying about paying the bills or customers leaving or other business issues Instead, you will be developing the habit of enjoying your life. When you start celebrating the little things, more and bigger things will begin happening for you, giving you more occasions to celebrate. The more you can celebrate the more fun you have, and the better you work and home life will be.

Drawing a Salary

Many business owners simply take all of the income that they get and then reinvest it back into growing their business or paying the bills. They end up not taking any money out as a salary for themselves. That is a dangerous precedent to set. You need to start drawing a salary from the very first day you are in business. I recommend drawing a percentage of revenue. For example, pay yourself 5% or 10% of revenue every month and put it into a separate bank account. You could treat that bank account as an emergency account if you would like but get into a habit of paying yourself

and not treating yourself as a free resource. When you
cost projects, put a price tag on your time at a rate that
reflects your value. As your business grows, any right-
hand person you hire as a replacement will require
compensation. If you are not drawing an equivalent
sum when you hire a right-hand person, you are going to
add a large expense to the company. This expense can
fundamentally impact the expense flow of your company.
By designing your business around this necessary expense
and drawing a real salary, you will be able to replace
yourself without negatively impacting your accounting.

Switching Off

For most business owners including myself, thinking
about something other than work can be difficult. But to
develop a balance in your life, you need to be able to come
home from work, and say, "enough is enough. I am not
going to think about work." This can be very difficult for
most people to understand, but you need to get into the
habit of just letting go of whatever issues are pressing at
work. Some people essentially "drop them off" by writing
outstanding issues down on a piece of paper and saying,
"I will let it go for now, I am at home. I will relax, turn
off my mobile phone, and turn my attention to my home
and family." If you adopt this technique, you will have
a much better home life. Six o'clock or seven o'clock in
the morning or whenever you start work, switch back on
again and concentrate on work. If you develop this work
mode and home mode distinction, you will generally have
a better work-life balance.

Work/Life Balance Tools

To achieve work-life balance several very effective tools
can assist you in starting and maintaining a distinct

work mode and home mode. One very useful technique involves time management. There are many time management tools out there and essentially, they all work... if you follow them. Time management tools may fail for many people because instead of implementing an entire system and staying with it, they pick up a diary system, or a computer system, or some other sort of time management idea, use it for about a month and then they stop using it. Six months down the road, they have regressed back to their old ways and are no longer managing their time well. The following tools all work extremely well. I can recommend them because I use them, have found them interesting and tend to stay with them over time.

"Getting Things Done"

The first tool is a book called "Getting Things Done" by David Allen. I have mentioned this previously and want to reiterate that this book has some unbelievably good ideas about managing time. One of the key ideas it proposes is to concentrate on the next action. Define the next thing that you can do to move an idea or some work forward. If you cannot think immediately of what your next action should be, then procrastination tends to set in. What "Getting Things Done" helps you do is divide all your work into projects. Projects are simply groups of actions. Once you define a project, at your next designated planning and thinking time, determine what your next actions will be to advance that project. You may have twenty projects that you have written down in separate files or folders, but the best way to move your projects forward is to concentrate on one project at a time. Get things done that are related to that project up into the point that you cannot move it forward any further then move on to the next project.

Time Chunking or Time Blocking

To manage my time effectively, I "time chunk," or "time block." This just means that I block out some time just for a particular project in advance. I go into my diary typically on a Friday night and I look at the next week. I start designating time, or pre-blocking time for certain activities that I need to accomplish or certain projects that must get done before the end of the week.

Top Six

Another tool that I use when appropriate helps me identify and focus on the top six items that I need to get done today. I repeat this process for tomorrow, the next day and the rest of the week. All you need to do then, is just look at the top six items you have prioritised and then have a list of everything else that you would like to get done. As long as you concentrate on getting the top six tasks done first, then you are free to do whatever you want for the rest of the day. Again, this comes back to the philosophy that you are only productive for two or three hours per day. The key is to maximize your productivity time to work on things that are important. For this, you need to be able to identify what is important. What do you have to get done? Block out the time to do those things. Once those critical items are accomplished, you are free to do all the other stuff. Sure enough, the day will fill up with stuff anyway. Things just happen and must be addressed. These tools: "Getting Things Done," time chunking, and the top six are all very effective and if you integrate them into your day, you will see the benefits immediately.

E-Mail Management

E-mail is one of the greatest time wasters I encounter in my day. Despite its convenience and value, it can be disruptive. The instant communication aspect of e-mail infers that as soon as a message comes in, you are expected to open it, address it and respond. If you have blocked out time to focus on an important task, this intrusion can be distracting. In reality, e-mail is often just busy work. It may relate to other issues you should address, but should not take priority.

My suggestion is to cut down the number of times you retrieve e-mail to only twice per day. For example, you could check e-mail first thing in the morning when you come in, and again when you get back from lunch. Limit yourself to only two times a day to retrieve, process, file and address issues in your e-mail. Allow yourself a specific amount of time for e-mail, then go and do your top six items. Do not get sucked into looking at e-mail every thirty minutes or every hour, or worse yet, every time you are notified of an e-mail message arriving. If you can reduce this task to only once per day, that is even better. There are certain situations where you must check your e-mail frequently, such as if you are working with an associate on a project and are e-mailing back and forth to coordinate your work. In such cases, look only at the e-mails that concern your project and either filter or disregard the rest until your designated e-mail session. The key is to stay focused and keep your priorities organised.

There is a book out at the moment called the "4-Hour Work Week," in which the author Tim Ferris suggests that you only look at email once per week. He suggests that he is more productive looking at e-mail once per week than he would be looking at it once per hour. There is a basic assumption underlying this philosophy. If you only need to look at your e-mail once per week, chances are you have a team of people that keep your business functioning for you. In such cases, you don't have to be there making decisions and adding to the mix of e-mails. You can achieve this independence from e-mail when you have your business systemised. The more that you can systemise your business, the more you can keep work moving through your business without you having to be present. The side benefit is the reduction in the amount and urgency of e-mail you receive.

12
Bringing It All Together

THE key to almost every issue in business from getting your personal time organised for maximum efficiency to preserving and building your equity in your business lies in systems. In the chapter on systemising, I gave you a "jump start" on how to begin systemising your business. This methodology works wonders on developing your thinking about how you can streamline your business. When it comes to more complex business issues however, it helps to have some assistance. To determine whether or not you should take your systemisation process further, I will give you an overview of what you can achieve, and hopefully answer some questions you may have.

When you start a business, you do so for your own reasons, but it is usually to achieve a certain freedom and lifestyle which comes from being the boss. It's a sad fact however, that the majority of businesses don't ever result in making a lot of money for the owner. Often it only provides a mediocre job for the owner until they want to retire. Unfortunately as we have already covered, when a business owner wants to retire, they find that they have few options. Most the options don't include selling their business and regaining their lifetime investment of time and money. For this reason, my entire approach is focused on getting a business in shape to sell it.

You will nearly always make more money when you sell the business than you ever make by working in the business. So, the underlying tenet of my thinking is that when you start a business, you start it with the intention of building your business in order to sell it. If you begin to think in those terms too, you will start to look at building value into your business. Again, as we have already discussed, if you increase the value of your business you will massively increase the amount of money that you receive when you sell it. I need to stress that you do not actually have to sell your business once you have it ready for sale. Your exit strategy may be to hand your business off to a member of your family. Your legacy is not worth much however, if it is simply a poorly packaged job with little long term value.

In the private equity world a group of investors will invest money in a business, take it over and change the business with the sole aim of selling it. For them, it is a purely financial transaction. When they buy a business, a private equity company typically wants businesses that can achieve six to seven times cash flow. They will buy it cheap and make changes to build up the value of the business to six to seven times the cash flow and then sell it. Most often, this can be achieved within two to five years.

Since you already have a business, are you thinking in those terms? Are you thinking about how you can massively increase the value of the business so that when you sell it, you get a huge amount of money for it and just cash in?

I am going to use an old example of an extremely systemised business: McDonalds.
McDonalds of course is an international franchise, but

if we just wind back a little bit we can understand what makes McDonalds valuable. To start with, Ray Kroc, who started McDonalds, never actually worked a day in a McDonald's store. He was a salesman who sold milkshake agitating machines. The McDonald brothers in Chicago had a hamburger store and they happened to sell a lot of milkshakes. Ray Kroc went to visit the McDonald brothers to see who was buying all the milkshake machines and he saw lines and lines of people waiting to buy hamburgers. He thought, "Hey, this is a good idea." And looked at how they were doing it. His amazing contribution to the business world was to come up with the idea of developing a system that he could use to repeat exactly what the McDonald brothers did. He could then sell that system to other storeowners and have them execute the exact same process. He started the first real franchise.

But some franchises today forget what they need to be really valuable... it is because of the systems. The power of McDonald's is the fact that a teenager with less than a high school education can run the store. Everything in the store is completely systemised, and standardised and runs from templates. Employees do not have to think about how to do something in that store, they just follow the predefined procedure and it just works as a system. Now is this approach really creative? Is it really flexible? Well, you could argue that it isn't, but it is very successful. It is very repeatable and very scalable and that is where the money lies.

Why Would You Systemise Your Business?

For many people, the concept of the perfect business is one that operates with very few skilled staff, that grows automatically, even while the owner is overseas on holiday and that can scale and take on more and more customers. In many ways, the ONLY way you could EVER get close to this is by implementing systems.

Systems allow a business to produce consistent and high quality work, with very little reliance on any individual person. Putting focus on systems, allows the business to improve efficiency and effectiveness. Errors are reduced, bottlenecks are exposed and redundancy is eliminated. All in all, a greater level of cost consciousness comes about. Reducing costs while keeping quality high allows for more sales and therefore more profits. The business becomes more scalable or has the ability to take on more staff and have them quickly and easily trained on how the business works. The business can react quickly to market demands and increased volume.

In this way alone, systems give a business a huge competitive advantage. They allow the business to be valued much higher than their competitors and gain a higher resale price. There is little or no downside to systemising a business.

Can You Systemise Everything?

There are a few areas where systemisation doesn't make sense for a business. Some of the more highly skilled areas that have key staff, are difficult to systemise. Areas that are artistic, creative or intuition-based are also more difficult.

One of the steps in my Business Autopilot System helps you identify the areas of the business that can be systemized. This is usually the majority of aspects of your business, but even when you find areas of your business that don't look like they can be systemised, there are usually many core functions surrounding and supporting that area that can definitely be systemised.

Is It Worth Trying To Systemise Everything?

In the end, your business is completely a reflection of the goals and aspirations you hold for it and for your life. With my Business Autopilot System process, you design how much or how little you want to systemise your business to achieve the most benefit and meet your goals.

The Jump Start process I've outlined in this book gives you all the elements you need to get started, and is an important part of the Autopilot system. If you want to take your business to the next step, consider investigating my full my Business Autopilot System.

There are several elements to the total system including complete support and expert advice and guidance which will help you achieve the maximum benefits for your entire business. As you step through the process, different approaches are suggested that are unique to your particular situation and position. You can take this "Full Autopilot" approach and follow all the steps to the letter completing everything as suggested. This approach provides the biggest long term benefits. You can also take a scaled down "Partial Autopilot" approach which selectively looks at your business to determine specific areas to systemise. This partial approach enables you to identify the areas which would benefit the most from systemising and allow you to concentrate on just those aspects of your business. You can also take a combined approach depending upon what works best for you.

With the benefit of expert guidance in this area you can have your business completely systemised and earning maximum profits in as little as six months. For business owners that are nearing retirement, or need to turn their business into an amazingly profitable enterprise as quickly as possible, there is no substitute for this expert guidance. Any costs are quickly amortised and the return on investment will far exceed your expectations.

For more information on my *Business Autopilot System*:

call: 1300-72-1995
fax: 02-8915-1544
email: info@systemised.com
web: www.Systemised.com

Business Autopilot Evening Seminar

"Would You Rather Own a Business Worth $200,000 or $2,000,000 – Learn How With This Proven System"

Sometimes we cannot get out of our own way when it comes to running a successful business. This evening seminar highlights where you might be causing your own problems. It then focuses on how to remove yourself as the problem and start transforming your business to one that runs on Autopilot.

Here are a few of the things you will learn and master:

- How to eliminate frustrations you have in your business
- The four steps you must make to guarantee that your ideas will be implemented
- Why knowledge and skill do not create wealth
- How to reset your business processes to automatically work for you
- How to use outsiders to accelerate your business growth And much more!

By the end of this seminar, you will re-ignite your passion for your business. You will know exactly how to make your business financially successful.

Visit http://www.Systemised.com for more information, seminar dates and to register for a seminar near you.

Business Autopilot 2-Day Workshop

"Put your Business on Autopilot – so you never have to work again"

This ground-breaking event is the companion to the Business Autopilot System™. All businesses deserve to serve the owner and its employees, but frequently they do not. Is your business giving you mediocrity, failure, struggle, ups and downs or is it successful, easy, providing a steady income and growing in value?

Here are a few of the things you will learn and master:
- Specific clearing processes to make space for greater success
- Why focusing on systems will set you free
- How to eliminate and remove frustrations
- Mapping out your business to identify the most critical areas for improvement
- How to identify bottlenecks in your business
- Tap into innovation and create products/services that customers really want
- How to take profitable action
- What we can learn from an 800 year old Italian economist
- How to test each and every idea before wasting hard-earning money on duds
- Identify and install the key measures that tell you everything about your business' health

And much more!

If you are not 100% satisfied with your business, if you're not 100% satisfied with your net worth, if you're burnt out, if you're working hard and not moving ahead, if you're business is not living up to your original vision, then maybe it's time for some new strategies and different ways of thinking. This program is transformational. You will not be the same person going out as were coming in. If you want to blend piece of mind with business success, join us at the next Business Autopilot Workshop.

Owners of the Business Autopilot System gain FREE entry to this Workshop, but need to register to secure their place.

Additional seats are available for you to be able to witness the Autopilot approach in action - much like ring-side seats at your favourite event.

Visit http://www.AutpilotWorkshop.com for more information and to register for a seminar near you.

Testimonials

I wish I'd known about this a lot sooner...

Simply going through the 'Jump Start' identified a number of bottlenecks that were holding up my business. Even better, I was able to quickly identify what to do to solve the problems and put in place a system so they won't hold up my business in future.

I can see the enormous potential of the 'Business Autopilot' to free up my time and help me breakthrough the roadblocks that have held back my business in the past. I wish I'd know about this a lot sooner!.

-Rashid Kotwal, Membership Website Guru, NSW, (02) 9499-7958

His approach has already freed up a large amount of my time...

"I'm so glad I was introduced to Murray and the 'Business Autopilot System'. Applying just one of the steps from the 'Jump-start' has already freed up a large amount of my time. I now have more time to build relationships with my clients and more time at home with my family. I highly recommend the Autopilot approach."

-Clare Monkley, CME Loans, Mortgage Broker
Central Coast, NSW

Visit http://www.Systemised.com for more information on the Business Autopilot System